How to Thrive as a
Library Professional

ACRL/NY Symposium 2020

How to Thrive as a Library Professional

ACHIEVING SUCCESS AND SATISFACTION

Susanne Markgren and Linda Miles

Shu —

Cheers to a successful and satisfying career!

LM + SM

LIBRARIES UNLIMITED®

An Imprint of ABC-CLIO, LLC

Santa Barbara, California • Denver, Colorado

Library of Congress Cataloging-in-Publication Data

Names: Markgren, Susanne, 1971– author. | Miles, Linda (Librarian), author.
Title: How to thrive as a library professional : achieving success and satisfaction / Susanne
    Markgren and Linda Miles.
Description: Santa Barbara, California : Libraries Unlimited, an imprint of ABC-CLIO,
    LLC, 2020. | Includes bibliographical references and index. |
Identifiers: LCCN 2019031263 (print) | LCCN 2019031264 (ebook) | ISBN 9781440867118
    (paperback : acid-free paper) | ISBN 9781440867125 (ebook)
Subjects: LCSH: Library science—Vocational guidance. | Library
    employees—Employment. | Library employees—Problems, exercises, etc. |
    Career development—Problems, exercises, etc.
Classification: LCC Z682.35.V62 M343 2020 (print) | LCC Z682.35.V62 (ebook) |
    DDC 020.23—dc23
LC record available at https://lccn.loc.gov/2019031263
LC ebook record available at https://lccn.loc.gov/2019031264

ISBN: 978-1-4408-6711-8 (paperback)
        978-1-4408-6712-5 (ebook)

24 23 22 21 20   1 2 3 4 5

This book is also available as an eBook.

Libraries Unlimited
An Imprint of ABC-CLIO, LLC

ABC-CLIO, LLC
147 Castilian Drive
Santa Barbara, California 93117
www.abc-clio.com

This book is printed on acid-free paper ∞

Manufactured in the United States of America

Contents

CHAPTER 6
Finding Your Place: Mindfulness and Self-Compassion 99

CHAPTER 7
Discovering Your True Purpose: Reflective Practice *115*

Acknowledgments

We are indebted to Barbara Ittner, who believed in us from the beginning, and to our editor, Jessica Gribble, who brought us to the finish line. Thank you to our colleagues: Jill Cirasella, Maureen Clements, Jeremy Czerw, Julia Furay, Christine Anne George, Amy Handfield, Sharon Jorrin, Gina Levitan, Kate Lyons, Carrie Marten, Jane Suda, Lisa Tappeiner, Eamon Tewell, Sharell Walker, Susan Wengler, and Haruko Yamauchi, who generously and graciously provided us with feedback or other assistance, and a special thank you to Kate Adler and the amazing Rena Grossman for their most valuable contributions. Without our partners, families, and closest colleagues, our vision would never have come to fruition. Special thanks to staff of An Beal Bocht Café, the Bronx watering hole where much of our collaboration unfolded. We are profoundly grateful for all the support.

Introduction

In the measurement world, you set a goal and strive for it. In the universe of possibility, you set the context and let life unfold.
                                                        —Zander and Zander (2002, p. 21)

Dority (2016) defines a successful career as one that is agile, opportunistic, sustainable, and meaningful (p. 212). In considering the direction and trajectory you might want for your career, Dority suggests, among other things, that you think carefully about who you are, who you can be, and who you want to be; that you come to understand and accept change; that you become skilled at spotting opportunity, anticipating what might come, and are willing to take risks; and that you are committed to continuous learning and develop an ability and willingness to continually reinvent yourself (pp. 7–9). These are important competencies that can assist us as we build our practices and grow as professionals.

The term *professional practice* holds many meanings. At a base level, it refers to practice in the sense of repetition—the tasks we do over and over to accomplish our work and support our patrons. We research information, acquire and organize resources, market library materials and services, teach patrons, answer questions, collaborate, innovate, improve, and lead library organizations. These actions are built upon skills we have developed through formal training and experience. We enact them repeatedly. We *practice (v.)* them. And as we develop these skills, *our practice (n.)* evolves and develops as well—it unfolds. One's professional practice could be considered spatially, encompassing the entirety of a realm of activity or influence. In this sense, a librarian's *practice* comprises all the tasks, responsibilities, collegial and supervisory relationships, patrons served, professional networks, and scholarly or creative work generated. *In practice* is also where theory becomes grounded in the real world—where we apply what we have learned in real situations in real libraries with real

1

colleagues and patrons, where the rubber meets the road, so to speak. Sometimes it seems as if the work we do just happens; the skills, tasks, and relationships to which we have become accustomed carry us along almost without our needing to think about practice, in any sense of the word. But what if we took a more deliberative approach to cultivating a practice? What if we hit the pause button and really examined our own individual careers and aspirations, the paths we've taken to get to where we are, and the direction in which we are headed?

This book focuses on what *professional practice* means for working librarians—the tasks we do routinely to support our patrons, the realm of influence in which we operate, and "where the rubber hits the road" as theory and action come together in the workplace. We cover a range of topics that are key to professional success, including figuring out where you want to go in your career and how to get there; cultivating multilateral relationships; understanding and successfully navigating organizational culture; developing proactive habits; using narrative and storytelling to define yourself as a professional, to advance your priorities, and to get the work done; employing mindfulness and self-compassion to support well-being and satisfaction; and practicing reflectively with an eye toward continual growth. Each chapter offers discussion, concrete examples, practical advice, exercises, and insights from a variety of fields of study, including psychology, education, health, sociology, and business.

Each chapter can stand on its own, and readers are encouraged to explore at their own pace and navigate by following their own curiosity and current needs. In the first chapter, on developing a vision for your career and a path forward, you will be introduced to five professional personas, giving you a taste of what librarianship is like, day to day, in different contexts. Joy is a branch manager in a public library, Marcus is a school librarian, Amir works in a special library in the financial services industry, Sana works at a small liberal arts college, and Camila is an archivist for a literary society. Throughout the book, we will rely on these personas to provide concrete examples of some of the challenges and practices discussed. These people are composites, their experiences and attitudes drawn from those of people we have met along our own professional journeys or pulled from situations and obstacles and relationships we've experienced ourselves. Their individual stories help to illustrate specific circumstances, as well as problems, actions, and solutions. We've attempted to design the persona narratives in any given chapter to stand on their own. However, it may be helpful to glance at the Boots on the Ground section of Chapter 1, where the personas are first introduced, to get a sense of each librarian and their role and background, before reading (or jumping around in) the remaining chapters. On the whole, the discussion and advice presented in this book are relevant to all librarians, no matter the type of institution where you practice or where you are in your journey. Students working toward a career in librarianship will be particularly rewarded.

What we have produced is what we've been calling "a professional development title" aimed at librarians, but in a broader sense, it falls within the genre of self-help literature that some have traced back as far as ancient Egypt and, in its modern incarnation, since the middle of the nineteenth century (Lee, 2017). A number of contemporary scholars have critiqued the self-help genre and related discourses (e.g., Gill & Orgad, 2018; Lee, 2017; Maasen, 2007; Rimke, 2000). The world according to self-help is all about marketplace supply and demand, where sages peddle quick fixes to consumers in need and who are more or less flying solo, striving for success or prosperity or for more vital things such as health, physical or psychological recovery, emotional well-being, or the meaning of life. Perhaps in every instance, they are searching for hope and optimism. They might benefit most at these times in their lives from a deep, nuanced wrestling match with complex questions and issues, but the marketplace of self-help instead offers a flattened, two-dimensional solution: just try it our way; just try harder.

In this supremely individualistic economy, each person is responsible for their own growth and development—not to mention success or failure. Both responsibility and blame rest with the individual subject, and scant attention is given to the constraining role of the structures within which we all live and toil. Aside from the absence of structural critique, certain tropes—such as time management as panacea—relentlessly championed, encourage voluntary, lifelong self-exploitation (Lee, 2017). This work on the self is not necessarily easy. The sheer weight of excessive self-responsibility and the compulsion to succeed at the highest level, at all costs, can be quite a burden. Willingness, drive, resilience, and relentlessness are idealized, and individuals who cannot successfully manage themselves—via the self-governance implicit in self-help—must be psychically or spiritually deficient; this is a *moral* failing (Rimke, 2000, p. 65). Ironically, hyper-self-positivity is rewarded in this bleak paradigm, as the subject is exhorted to embrace the upbeat outlook of glass-half-full. The concept of resilience, or the ability to "bounce back," recover, and move forward whenever failure or setbacks are experienced, is problematic in itself (e.g., Gill & Orgad, 2018), and scholars are beginning to examine this phenomenon as it plays out in libraries as well (e.g., Berg, Galvan, & Tewell, 2018; Levesque & Skyrme, 2019).

Yet we would be loath to discourage the drive for success out of hand, and there's no doubt that practical advice and "lessons learned" from those who've gone before can be instrumental for positive professional and career development. Librarians, in particular, seem to place a lot of value on assisting new librarians and those taking on new responsibilities or seeking to advance within the profession. Lee (2017) suggests counteracting the negative effects of self-help discourse by equipping individuals for critical reflection on their own learning and its contexts (pp. 158–159). In this volume, we attempt to do so by including this introduction to the challenges posed by the genre, and we encourage readers to engage with some of the literature on the topic listed at the end of this introduction. At various points in the narrative of striving and self-improvement that you will encounter in this book, we hope you'll find ample opportunities to think critically about the world of work, our institutions, your own local context, and how you fit in there.

This book grew out of a love for what we do and a passion for helping others discover and cultivate pathways to successful, satisfying, and thriving professional careers. We, the authors, have been working librarians for more than thirty years combined. We work in different libraries, in different roles, and have different backgrounds, experiences, and skills. Yet we have collaborated over the years on developing a variety of professional development opportunities for students, job seekers, and librarians (both new and seasoned). Continuously since 2012, Linda, as cochair of the New Librarians Discussion Group of the Greater New York Chapter of the Association of College and Research Libraries (ACRL/NY), and Susanne, as head of the Mentoring Program, have organized panels and workshops that covered navigating the job search and hiring process, the first days/weeks/months/years on the job, and building relationships and networks, among other topics. We have collaborated with colleagues on a research and writing support group and have facilitated workshops for the Placement and Career Development Service of the American Library Association (ALA). Along the way we've enjoyed hundreds of collegial relationships and participated in thousands of conversations about becoming a professional and building a practice. In recent years, we've witnessed a growing demand for programming to assist people with some of the challenges and struggles they feel as they seek direction and meaning in the profession, adapt to new roles, go up for promotion or tenure, or simply work to find a job. Many of the concepts, exercises, and questions that are included in this book grew out of our collaborative programming.

Something that separates professional fulfillment from mere enjoyment of the work may be in the relationship between you and the work itself—how you engage with it, how it makes you feel.

> Workers are [fully] engaged in their work when they are committed to a purpose, using their intelligence to make choices about how to best accomplish the task, monitoring their behavior to make sure they are doing the task well, checking to make sure their actions are actually accomplishing the purpose, and taking corrective action when needed. (Thomas, 2009, p. 38)

This sense of autonomy and direction over one's own practice is the hallmark of a professional career. Purpose, passion, and self-reflection play key roles in determining direction, but actively taking ownership, responsibility, or agency may be what truly defines professional level work. Tymon and Thomas (2009) propose engagement with active decision-making as among the four key factors for intrinsic motivation, referring specifically to decisions about where to invest one's time and effort, and approaches to accomplishing the work.

In the end, drawing from Dority (2016), agility, meaningfulness, and sustainability are our goals. With conceptual framing, reflective prompts, and action-oriented exercises, this book delves deeply into specific elements of a librarian's practice, helps individuals connect the material to their own professional lives, and helps prepare them for action. Readers will be prompted to consider new ways of thinking about their current practice and where they want to go. Librarians at all stages (in training through veteran and anywhere in between) and those working in all library contexts will discover a cohesive pathway toward building a successful professional practice while opening a world of new possibilities.

REFERENCES

Berg, J., Galvan, A., & Tewell, E. (2018). Responding to and reimagining resilience in academic libraries. *Journal of New Librarianship, 3*(1), 1–4.

Dority, G. K. (2016). *Rethinking information work: A career guide for librarians and other information professionals.* Santa Barbara, CA: Libraries Unlimited.

Gill, R., & Orgad, S. (2018). The amazing bounce-backable woman: Resilience and the psychological turn in neoliberalism. *Sociological Research Online, 23*(2), 477–495.

Lee, M. (2017). Decoding the neoliberal subjectivity in self-helping adult learners. *International Journal of Lifelong Education, 36*(1–2), 145–163.

Levesque, L., & Skyrme, A. E. (2019). New librarians and the practice of everyday life. *Canadian Journal of Academic Librarianship, 5,* 1–24.

Maasen, S. (2007). Governing by will: The shaping of the will in self-help manuals. In M. Ash & T. Sturm (Eds.), *Psychology's territories: Historical and contemporary perspectives from different disciplines* (pp. 111–128). Mahwah, NJ: Lawrence Erlbaum.

Rimke, H. M. (2000). Governing citizens through self-help literature. *Cultural studies, 14*(1), 61–78.

Thomas, K. W. (2009). *Intrinsic motivation at work: What really drives employee engagement.* San Francisco, CA: Berrett-Koehler.

Thomas, K. W., & Tymon, W. G., Jr. (2009). *Work engagement profile.* Mountain View, CA: CPP.

Zander, R. S., & Zander, B. (2002). *The art of possibility.* New York, NY: Penguin Books.

1

Forging a Path: Career Vision

A vision is a big purpose—a daring and inspiring image of a future that you want to create.

—Thomas (2009, p. 98)

Joy is the manager of a public library branch in a medium-sized city. In addition to managing a budget, overseeing operations, and supervising staff, she gets to take on special projects related to areas of particular interest to her—for instance, putting together a summer program designed to encourage girls' interest in technology and design. She is very proud of what she and her staff have accomplished, has built a network of collegial relationships with other professionals, and really looks forward to going to work every day. She honestly can't imagine herself anywhere else. But Joy is a second-career librarian, having taken a long path through two very different landscapes. After graduating from college, she was happy to leave academia behind but wasn't really sure where she wanted to go. She took a position doing digital design work with the firm where she had completed her senior internship. Joy more or less "fell into" this opportunity, finding the work fast paced and enjoyable. For a little over ten years, she moved from project to project garnering both personal satisfaction and the respect of colleagues. Unfortunately, the company didn't survive in the long run, and she found herself at loose ends once again.

For Joy, this was an opportunity to take a break, breathe, and very deliberately think about where she wanted to go next. She took stock of what she really loved about the type of work she had been doing, along with the kinds of things she liked to do outside of work. She thought about her personality, what she found rewarding, challenging, and frustrating about her previous position, and contemplated different types of industries and opportunities that might provide success and fulfillment for someone with her background, talents, and desires. Librarianship was one of the career paths that stood out to her. She remembered how much she enjoyed going to libraries as a child and spending time there while in college. She learned more about the profession and the wide range of career options that librarianship offered. Once she had enough information to understand the different kinds of potential roles and institutions, the day-to-day work, and the variety of patrons and clientele and communities served in the profession, Joy knew that she ultimately wanted to take on a leadership role in a public library. After choosing a destination, she considered the skills, experiences, and credentials that she might need to get there. Finally, she focused on what she wanted to do next. She was ready.

Developing a vision and taking meaningful steps on the path toward that vision are exercises rooted in commitment and action. Whether you're a student just beginning to think about your future as a working professional or, like Joy, you're looking for a new path and wondering if there's a different position in your future, developing a sense of where you want to go and visualizing a path forward may help you do the best, most energized, and rewarding work of your professional life. This chapter will help you build self-awareness: What do you know about yourself as a professional or professional-to-be? What work is most meaningful for you? As you contemplate these questions, it is important to visualize a destination: Whom will you work with? As a librarian, what constituency will you serve or support? What will you help them accomplish? Would you find more fulfillment in a focused specialization or working on an eclectic range of projects? Building an effective professional career also requires deliberate action. How will you use your time and energy to reach that destination? What are the first steps on the path that will allow you to cultivate the future you envision? This chapter will get you moving in the direction that's right for you.

VISION, ACTION, AND MOMENTUM

People who take the plunge, who commit themselves to going after what they really want, often . . . begin to attract to themselves the knowledge, relationships, and resources they require to accomplish their work.
—Boldt (2004, p. 23)

A vision is a goal. It is not yet realized, but it provides a coherent, if not fully concrete, sense of somewhere you want to be—in this case doing something you want to do, collaborating with people you can imagine working next to you, and serving patrons, institutions, and communities deserving of your energy and commitment. Your professional vision involves at least three things: (1) you—doing work well matched to your talents, interests, and values; (2) one or more organizations, institutions, or partnerships, providing the context for your professional practice; and (3) in the library world, a community of patrons who will benefit from your efforts. There are plenty of people in our profession who have become successful doing what they love to do. For some, getting to such a place is the result of fortunate happenstance: "I just lucked into my dream job." This is similar to the way Joy found fulfillment in her initial career, by "falling into" it. It does happen, sometimes. For the rest of us, at least some measure of vision and planning is useful. It's also not always a straight line from where we are now to where we hope to land; the journey may involve a series of challenges and obstacles.

The passage by Laurence Boldt, at the start of this section, suggests the power of vision. When you develop and commit to a vision for your future, things that can support your success begin to coalesce around you. Thomas (2009) similarly suggests that "if [your vision] is daring, the excitement of that future possibility will begin to pull you forward, and you will begin finding ways to make it happen" (p. 98). There is a certain level of momentum in a journey with a destination. A clear idea of where you may want to ultimately land, at the very least, can make you more primed to recognize and take advantage of the kinds of training, experiences, and relationships that could help move you along that sometimes rocky path.

The path to career fulfillment will be different for everyone, because individuals are motivated differently. Some argue that fulfilling work is inherently intrinsically motivated. In other words, you may be less motivated by external conditions, such as salary or acclaim (although these are also valuable considerations), and more dedicated to doing something for internal reasons. For Gini (2000), this means that a fulfilled worker is *impelled* to engage, in the way that children feel *a need* to play (p. xii). Some workers are motivated by what is commonly referred to as "a sense of purpose" or, in other words, something beyond the internal/external dichotomy. They are professionally engaged in something that makes life better for humanity or satisfies specific needs of others (p. xii). For many, this is a working Life with a capital *L*. According to Thomas (2009), "Much of the color in our lives comes from the drama, challenge, struggle—and it is hoped the triumph—of handling the uncertainties involved in accomplishing those purposes" (p. 21). The level of energy attached to this kind of purposeful engagement may be appropriately referred to as "a passion for. . .," going well beyond simple alignment with one's values (p. 51).

THE START

Just where you are—that's the place to start.

—Chödrön (1994, p. 34)

Reflecting on where you are now and how you got here is an important first step in the visioning process. It's also important to realize that there's nothing wrong with changing your vision as you progress along your path. In fact, it's expected. We evolve as professionals all the time, as do our institutions, communities, and patrons' needs and interests. It is wise to periodically carve out opportunities to reflect on where you've been so that you can reaffirm or adjust your path. Vision development is not merely for the student, newly minted, or novice librarian; this kind of work can and should play a role throughout one's career. Let's start with an initial assessment of where you are right now in your professional practice.

EXERCISE: CURRENT CONTEXTS

Characterize the following elements. If you are not currently working in a library, for instance, if you're working temporarily in a bank or if you're a student whose "work" takes place in a library school program, consider *that* the "context" you are analyzing here. This is about establishing a sense of where you are now, wherever that may be.

The Workplace

	"Just the facts" description	Best adjectives to describe
Location		
Physical space		
Character, feel, atmosphere		
Overall worker satisfaction		

Colleagues

	"Just the facts" description	Best adjectives to describe
How do individuals work together?		
Supervisory/collegial relationships		
Your and others' habitual practices		

The Organization

	"Just the facts" description	Best adjectives to describe
Goals/mission (on paper)		
Goals/mission (in practice, from your perception)		

The Target Audience (Clients, Patrons, Customers, Beneficiaries)

	"Just the facts" description	Best adjectives to describe
Whom does the organization serve?		
What does the organization help them accomplish?		
Whom do you deal with beyond organizational members?		

Finally, address the following questions in a journal: Where do you see yourself, right now, in this context? What is your role? What do you do? Whom do you interact with? How do you feel about the elements you've identified and characterized? Are there things you love? Hate? Feel indifferent to?

A greater awareness of your current context, where you are beginning your journey, is the first step toward envisioning the road forward.

Once you've reflected a bit on your current context, the next step is to do a little self-reflection. For Arthur, Khapova, and Richardson (2017), agency—the ability to move forward and accomplish purposeful goals—is dependent first and foremost on self-knowledge (p. 17). What do you know about who you are—right here, right now? It might be useful to do a skills and knowledge self-assessment, such as a SWOT analysis (thinking explicitly about Strengths, Weaknesses, Opportunities available to you, and Threats to eventual success), and, indeed, you may want to take this up as a later project. But here we're going to focus on something a bit more elemental: your identity. How do you think about yourself, and how does that differ from the way others see you?

Thinking critically about where you are now, how you got there, and how you see yourself as a professional prepares you for looking to the future.

BOOTS ON THE GROUND: WHAT THE WORK LOOKS LIKE

Though your first thought of librarianship may be of people sitting behind a desk waiting to answer a question or check out a book, this image barely begins to represent the vast array of work within libraries.

—Pressley (2009, p. 8)

Now that you've reflected on where you are and who you are, and what's most important to you as a professional or a developing professional, we'll take a look at a range of possibilities for a career in librarianship.

Public Librarian

Joy is a branch manager in a public library. Her institution is part of a county library system that provides information, resources, and services to the community. Public libraries are usually positioned not only as a source of materials for learning and pleasure but also as a hub for the community, providing access to vital resources and services such as internet access and printing, information about social services in the community, and meeting space for local organizations. The library provides targeted programming for children, teens, adults, and seniors. Because the patron base is so wide and varied, Joy has assembled a team of library professionals who provide collection development and programming for different segments of the population—for instance, young adults or seniors. While specific individuals head up efforts in each of these specialized areas, they are expected to support one another across the divisions. There are staff working alongside librarians to support access services, collection management, facilities maintenance, and other areas of work. Joy oversees branch operations, convenes cross-departmental meetings to help keep everyone informed about work in other areas, provides input on specific projects, is a liaison to central management of the library system, and, when she can carve out time to do so, is happy to personally manage initiatives that are nearest and dearest to her heart. Day to day, this means that she spends most of her time on the phone, in meetings, or at her computer. Sometimes she has to stop everything to attend to an unforeseen emergency. Early in her career as a public librarian, she was more on the front lines, interacting with patrons and colleagues, and she does miss this aspect but makes up for it as best she can when she gets to leave all the craziness behind to work with those technology-focused teens.

School Librarian

Marcus works in a public high school as a school librarian, or what is sometimes called a library media specialist. Like Joy, he came to librarianship as a second career, returning to graduate school to acquire his master of library science (MLS) degree after three years as a high school history teacher. Marcus really enjoys working with young people, supporting them through coursework and extracurricular activities, such as "mathletes," science fairs, and reading clubs. Moreover, he loves the fact that he gets to take on a leadership and advocacy role in the school and in the community. Keyed into the importance of written culture for young people's development, Marcus has been asked to speak locally about the importance of books and the practice of reading, both in school and at home. He has been leading a lobbying effort at his school to gain funding for so-called classroom libraries, collections of materials housed in the classroom and selected by teachers to meet the diverse needs of their students, academic and otherwise. He also works with local public librarians to develop progra:ming for young adults. Marcus's input on curriculum matters at the school is highly valued, and he is currently working with colleagues on a number of initiatives, including design of a social studies unit interweaving use of library resources with critical thinking activities, textbook material, and homework. Like most library media specialists, Marcus is a "solo librarian," wearing a lot of hats. A typical day might find him leading a hands-on information literacy workshop for an English class, meeting with a couple of teachers over lunch to discuss a media literacy project they're working on, spending some time evaluating databases for potential subscription, teaching student helpers how to locate and shelve books using the Dewey Decimal system, and hosting an after-school "big ideas" debate session.

Special Librarian

Amir is one of two librarians staffing an information center in a large financial services corporation. This kind of position, outside of public, academic, or school libraries, is generally referred to as a "special librarian." Other examples include librarians who work in hospitals, law firms, nonprofit organizations, and so forth. The primary mission of the corporation Amir works for is to provide wealth management and investment advice to clients, and the information center provides support for these activities in a number of ways. It is vital that financial services professionals stay up-to-date on financial and business news, and Amir is in charge of managing subscriptions to news and alert services, as well as reviewing news stories, abstracting, and distributing alerts himself via the corporate intranet. The information center also plays a key role in "competitive intelligence" work, investigating peer organizations to stay current on the plans and activities of competitors. Finally, the information center houses the archives of the corporation, managing retention, preservation of, and access to all kinds of records and data. He works very closely with one other librarian on staff and serves on teams with colleagues from across the organization on specific initiatives. On a given day, Amir gets to the office bright and early to review the news services and send any urgent alerts; takes a meeting with the head of his division, who expects updates on certain projects and provides direction for new initiatives; and participates in a meeting with colleagues from the technology division related to a new data archiving platform. Amir is proud of the respect he's gained among other professionals in the organization and most enjoys the leadership role he gets to play on certain projects. It is a hectic and high-stress environment, however, and Amir is first to admit that it's not for everyone.

Academic Librarian

Sana is a cataloging and acquisitions librarian at a small liberal arts college. The primary mission of her library is to support student learning and faculty teaching. Librarians in her institution have faculty status and are required to prove themselves in the areas of librarianship, research, and service to the institution over the course of a seven-year tenure track. While her primary responsibilities are in technical services, Sana is also a liaison to the faculty of the English department, providing collection development, information literacy instruction, and support for faculty. She is called upon to staff the reference desk at least one shift per week. One of the things Sana likes best about her job is that she interacts in meaningful ways with so many people—students at the reference desk and in the class-room, library colleagues working with her on specific initiatives, faculty in the English department who are working on research or publication, col-leagues from across the institution who serve with her on the campus-wide curriculum committee, and colleagues from other institutions who serve with her on a consortial collections management committee. A typical day may involve responding to emails from colleagues, faculty members, and her director; copy cataloging any new books that have come into the library; creating spending reports based on fund codes and departments; working a few hours at the reference desk; attending a virtual board meet-ing; and meeting with a colleague to develop a chapter proposal for an upcoming book. She absolutely loves all the things she does but also finds the pressure of it all more than a little bit overwhelming.

Archivist

Camila is an archivist who works for a literary society and has an aca-demic background in American literature. She is in charge of acquiring, preserving, describing, and providing access to literary artifacts, such as manuscripts, rare books, working papers, correspondence, and occasion-ally the personal belongings of authors or other luminaries. Like Amir, she is also charged with retention and preservation of the official records of the organization. Camila reports to the associate director and works closely with the curatorial staff, who determine collection priorities, and with the director of development to secure funding to acquire materials. In some cases, she is the primary contact for authors, estate managers, or collectors. She is the liaison to museum professionals around the world who borrow and display artifacts, and she supervises three interns plus one contract archivist who is working on a specific grant-funded project. She is an expert in the preservation and safe handling of artifacts. She and her small team catalog items using a standard industry schema, which is somewhat different from cataloging of traditional library materials. She serves as liaison with scholars who need to access the organization's col-lections to carry out research. An average day combines a lot of email and phone conversations with any number of individuals, planning meetings with curatorial staff, troubleshooting cataloging questions with team members, and careful handling of artifacts during the description process.

These situations share a number of characteristics—frankly, all five seem somewhat fast paced and/or pressurized, for example. But there are subtle differences. Sana, our academic librarian, is perhaps doing the widest range of different things—from technical services to public services to writing and publishing. Amir and Camila each focus on a specific realm of knowledge—business and economics for Amir and literature for Camila, as compared to Joy, Marcus, and Sana, whose libraries' collections presumably cover the wide universe of knowledge. On any given day, it seems that each of these individuals spends some time focusing and working alone and also meeting and collaborating with others. You may be able to imagine Joy happily shaking off her last meeting of the day so that she can sit down to teach basic coding to teens, Marcus introducing some of the new equipment the library has in its circulating technology collection to the members of the school photography club, Amir reviewing the overnight news feeds first thing in the morning to pull out the most vital information for his senior vice president, Sana meeting with a new English professor to talk about targeted library instruction for her students, and Camila training an intern who is attempting to describe Emily Brontë's embroidered handkerchief.

This is obviously a reductive sampling of the kinds of work that librarians do, and there are many more types of librarianship and information-related work out there. For instance, the work of a public librarian will vary significantly depending on the type of community served (e.g., urban versus rural, to name just one variable), and not all academic librarians are considered faculty, which can greatly impact what's expected of them and how they operate within their institutions. Then there are the generic variations between public service library work and technical services or access services or management. Not to mention the fact that these five individuals do many more and varied things than could possibly be captured in our description of a single "average day." These narratives are simply meant to provide a sense of the gritty day-to-day delights (and challenges!) in various types of library contexts. They are clearly portraits of librarians with very different traits and skills, taking on different kinds of work, in different contexts, but there are elements of each story that may help clarify those differences. These include workplace and culture, colleagues and relationships, organizations, the populations served or supported, and the nature of that service or support.

For anyone who is job seeking, or for anyone who may be thinking of changing their career, a worthwhile strategy is the *informational interview*. These types of informal interviews can help to illuminate the day-to-day reality in various roles and workplaces while at the same time exposing nuances and subtleties that may make a certain type of position appealing or unappealing—if you ask the right questions. They are a fantastic tool for the vision quest.

Informational interviews are essentially meetings with working professionals to facilitate an understanding of

- who they are,
- what they do,
- how their organization functions,
- how their work fits in with those operations,
- how they got to where they are now, and
- how they see the future of their particular sector of library-related work.

A key requirement for informational interviews is that they are purely informational and in no way an entreaty for future employment consideration. Assuring your interviewees of this condition ahead of time will help them feel more comfortable sharing their stories with you. These exchanges may provide opportunities for you to fill in any gaps you've identified in your working conception of a rewarding future while offering real-world perspectives from working individuals.

EXERCISE: INFORMATIONAL INTERVIEW QUESTIONS

Consider the following questions as you prepare for an informational interview. Adapt them as necessary, based on the specifics of the interviewee's situation.

1. What is your organization's mission?
2. For what types of patrons, users, or clients does your organization provide information and services? What are the primary needs of these constituencies?
3. Can you describe the structure of your organization (departments, units, reporting relationships)? Where do you fit into that picture?
4. What are your primary responsibilities? What kinds of activities do you take on, and what does that look like on an average day?
5. To what degree is what you do self-directed? In other words, how much freedom do you have in determining where you invest your time and effort?
6. What activities do you find most/least fulfilling, and why?

7. What role does creativity play in your work and that of your colleagues?
8. In what way, if any, does teamwork or collaboration play a role in your work? Could you briefly describe your most important workplace relationships?
9. What are the primary challenges for you, your colleagues, or your organization?

Although you'll go into the informational interview with a draft set of questions in mind, be sure to remain flexible. Interviews are somewhat organic, living and breathing in the moment. Practice the questions, but be ready to change things up depending on what comes out in conversation. In addition to providing critical insight about what it's like to work in a particular job or in a certain workplace, these interviews can provide meaningful networking relationships, which could support your career well beyond the initial stages.

Now that you've considered where you're starting from, what you bring to the table in terms of how you see yourself professionally, and what some professional practices "look like," it's time to begin building a vision of your own future context and future work. This is where the vision begins to take shape.

EXERCISE: FUTURE CONTEXT

The Workplace

	How important? (0 to 10) 10 = essential	Describe it
Location		
Physical space		
Character, feel, atmosphere		
Overall worker satisfaction		

Colleagues

	How important? (0 to 10) 10 = essential	Describe it
How do individuals work together?		
Supervisory/collegial relationships		
Your and others' habitual practices		

The Organization

	How important? (0 to 10) 10 = essential	Describe it
Goals/mission (on paper)		
Goals/mission (in practice)		

The Target Audience (Clients, Patrons, Customers, Beneficiaries)

	How important? (0 to 10) 10 = essential	Describe it
Whom does the organization serve?		
What does the organization help them accomplish?		
Whom do you deal with beyond organizational members?		

Filling out the details of your expectations regarding workplace, colleagues, organization, and patrons or clientele helps you understand where you want to land in your next position and why. Once an idea of future professional context has begun to take shape, it is time to consider the professional tasks, responsibilities, and relationships you may hope to tackle in this space. When you do this work that you care about so much, "what does success look like to you?" (Arthur, Khapova, & Richardson, 2017, p. 49). Among elements to consider are the types of responsibilities you may be taking on and the networks and types of professional relationships you will develop and sustain.

EXERCISE: FUTURE TASK/RESPONSIBILITY JOURNALING

In a journal, take some time to answer the following questions. There are no right or wrong ways to interpret these questions. Let your mind wander.

1. First, what is the passion that drives you? What matters?
2. What are the elements of success?
3. What are your priorities?
4. What kinds of activities will you take on, day to day?

5. What kinds of collegial, collaborative, supervisor-supervisee, or mentor-mentee relationships will be most important and rewarding?

6. What kinds of clients, users, patrons will you be working with? What kinds of interactions will you have with them?

7. In what ways will you be able to, or encouraged to, exercise agency over your own actions?

8. Would you find more fulfillment in a focused specialization or working on an eclectic range of projects?

9. In what ways or to what degree will you be personally responsible for the outcomes of your work?

This exercise is designed to take you beyond a superficial conception of where you may end up practicing your profession and get you down to the nitty-gritty of the most important elements of your work—to what's most important to *you*, that is. In addition, if you are thinking of setting up a few informational interviews, you may want to use the Future Context exercise and the Future Task/Responsibility exercise to help you figure out whom to reach out to and what kinds of questions to ask them.

Between and through these exercises, you have been developing a complex understanding of the future professional life you envision. You are armed with new understandings of yourself, the work you really want to do, and the immensity and diversity of librarianship itself. The next exercise provides an opportunity for you to identify potential gaps in that new vision. What do you still need to figure out?

EXERCISE: CONCEPT MAPPING

Develop a visual representation of a concept map with you at the center.

1. Draw a circle in the center of a piece of paper to represent yourself.

2. Draw additional circles on the page to represent different elements of the professional position you are envisioning. Include anything you can think of: workplace, organization, colleagues, patrons, tasks, responsibilities, what you do day to day.

3. Visually represent the relationships among concepts.

4. Add in any of the experiences, skills, or knowledge you may need to acquire in order to get where you want to go.

5. Identify any gaps in your visualization: what's missing? Are there areas of knowledge or experience that you can't yet visualize?

6. Follow-up "homework": do some research to chase down what's in those gaps.

This exercise can help concretize some of the career elements you've begun to think about throughout the previous exercises and can also bring to mind things that you hadn't previously considered.

MOVING FORWARD

Commitment is clearly more than desiring or hoping that the purpose will be achieved. It is a decision to take personal responsibility for making it happen.

—Thomas (2009, p. 31)

Now that you've developed a clear vision of where you want to go, it's time to plan. For Thomas and Tymon (2009), forward progress is one of the requirements for truly engaged and motivated work. Sustainability comes from knowing yourself, realizing the direction you want to take, and also mapping out those next steps. It is that initial mapping that we focus on now. How will you begin to develop the momentum you need to get where you want to go? How will you use your time and energy to reach that destination? What are the first steps on the path that will allow you to cultivate the future you envision? Arthur, Khapova, and Richardson (2017) list confronting and removing roadblocks as one of the hallmarks of an "intelligent career" (p. x). What are the strategies that will keep you moving past those unexpected bumps in the road? Flexibility, creativity, and considering contingencies in advance can help keep you on track.

EXERCISE: FIRST STEPS

In a journal, take some time to answer the following questions. There are no right or wrong ways to interpret these questions. Let your mind wander.

1. What are the formal credentials required for the kind of position you have envisioned? What is your plan for obtaining these, and what is the timeline?

2. Restate the responsibilities and skills from the Future Task/Responsibility exercise—which of these do you already have knowledge of and/or experience with? Which are you already on the way toward acquiring/accomplishing? Which will require formal training, and where might you access that? Which could be acquired/accomplished through experience, and where might you gain that experience?

3. Who are the individuals or types of individuals who might be instrumental in helping you along the way (e.g., people who could help you gain the skills/knowledge you need, people already working in that library sector or doing the kind of work you're most interested in,

people who are active collaborators with people who are doing that work)? Are there individuals you already have relationships with who fit these categories? Can you identify individuals who might fit the open categories? How might you make a connection and begin building a relationship?

4. How do people in that sector, doing that work, stay current? Are there ways you can begin monitoring or taking part in those trainings and discussions?

How do you know you're making progress? Finding fulfillment is an iterative process, and milestones set up along the way will establish points of reference and provide space for reflection and course correction. As you develop a mental model of the path you will take, it will be useful to sketch out a sequence of experiences or steps and then explicitly plan for specific moments of stillness—opportunities to temporarily stop focusing on forward momentum so that you can take a breath and consider any changes that have occurred. It is possible that practices in that specific sector of librarianship will have evolved or that the information and service needs of its patrons will have shifted—as the world turns, so to speak. But it is almost certain that *you* will have changed, too, as you have gained new experiences, built new relationships, and grappled with new challenges along the way. Professional vision should never be stagnant—the path will shift even as you are navigating it.

REFERENCES

Arthur, M. B., Khapova, S. N., & Richardson, J. (2017). *An intelligent career: Taking ownership of your work and your life.* New York, NY: Oxford University Press.

Boldt, L. G. (2004). *How to find the work you love.* New York: Penguin Compass.

Chödrön, P. (1994). *Start where you are: A guide to compassionate living.* Boston, MA: Shambhala.

Gini, A. (2000). *My job, my self: Work and the creation of the modern individual.* New York, NY: Routledge.

Pressley, L. (2009). *So you want to be a librarian.* Duluth, MN: Library Juice Press.

Thomas, K. W. (2009). *Intrinsic motivation at work: What really drives employee engagement.* San Francisco, CA: Berrett-Koehler.

Thomas, K. W., & Tymon, W. G., Jr. (2009). *Work engagement profile.* Mountain View, CA: CPP.

2

Gathering and Lending Support:
Relationships

No matter how brilliant you are at your job, if you want to get ahead, good relationships at work will help. Task awareness is fine, and being good at your job is eminently desirable. But, if you can harness that with being passionate about people, it will take you further, faster.

—Kay (2009, p. xiv)

Camila has been in her current position as archivist for a literary society and museum for two years, having gained prior experience working on various grant-funded projects at different cultural institutions. During a yearlong stretch between library school and her first job, and throughout the years of freelancing, she focused a lot on building confidence, developing a professional reputation, and making connections with working archivists. By the time she was hired on at the institute, she had taken part in a mentoring program sponsored by her alma mater, meeting and emailing with an experienced museum archivist, and participated on a committee planning the annual conference of a regional professional organization. The letters of recommendation that helped her get the job at the institute came from a previous employer, her mentor, and a couple of the more active members of that professional organization. Relationships continue to drive her success. For example, her supervisor helps her navigate the internal politics of the organization, the head curator provides encouragement and feedback related to the project proposals she's put forward for approval, and she has developed fast friendships with a couple of institute colleagues. The organization's professional staff support each other in many ways, and one of the things she loves most about her job is working collaboratively with others on multiple different projects, all at the same time. When she first arrived, Camila was asked to join an outreach initiative serving local high schools. This small, dedicated band of colleagues has become a coordinated and very effective team. In the broader professional community, she has continued to work hard to stay active within her professional organizations and maintain contacts with others she's met along the way, although she'd be the first to admit that she finds it tough, time- and energy-wise, to keep on top of it all. She's proud of the connections she's made so far in her career—there is the personal satisfaction she gets from these relationships, of course, but she also knows it's a smart way to build a successful professional practice.

Relationships can play important and varied roles in librarians' professional lives. They exist in many forms and at many levels. There are people we work closely with and those we may never meet in person. There are relationships we seek out and those that find us. They all have purpose and meaning. What roles can professional relationships play across a career? How do overlapping and networked relationships help an individual develop professionally, succeed, get ahead, and provide satisfaction and meaning? And what can a librarian do to foster these connections in their own practice? In this chapter, we consider the why, what, who, and how of networking and relationships.

WHY: FLOURISHING AT WORK

Nearly every day brings an opportunity to build the relationships that woven together make up your lifelong professional community. The key is to approach this not so much as an investment in your career success but rather as one of the richest rewards of life: being in a position to support others.

—Dority (2016, p. 176)

Traditionally, work relationships have been seen as important for helping individuals address specific task objectives or helping them to persevere through difficult and challenging stages of their careers. Colbert, Bono, and Purvanova (2016) posit a set of six work relationship functions, three of which have traditionally been associated with these relationships and three that they propose as part of a new, more holistic view of the potential impact of work relationships on individuals' lives. For Colbert's research team, work relationships not only function in support of individuals struggling with adversity, as implied in previous literature (e.g., Stroebe & Stroebe, 1996), but are also important for employee "flourishing," which implies additional positive effects for the individual (Table 2.1).

Surveying full-time workers from a variety of occupations, these researchers found that task assistance (one of the work relationship benefits traditionally studied), plus all three of their newly theorized benefits (friendship, personal growth, and opportunities to give to others), were each significantly related to at least one of the four positive outcomes of employee "flourishing." The other two traditional relationship benefits (career advancement and emotional support) were also positively, but not significantly, related to flourishing (Table 2.2).

Table 2.1   Functions and effects of work relationships. From Colbert, Bono, and Purvanova (2016).

Traditional functions of work relationships	Additional functions theorized by Colbert, Bono, and Purvanova (2016)	Effects of flourishing
Task assistance	Friendship	Job satisfaction
Career advancement (advice and sponsorship)	Personal growth and development	Positive emotions at work
Emotional support	Opportunities to support others	Life satisfaction
		More meaningful work

Table 2.2   Why network? From Colbert, Bono, and Purvanova (2016).

Type of relationship benefit	Positive outcome ("flourishing")
Feeling supported in specific tasks or objectives	Significant impact on job satisfaction
Friendship (enjoying each other's company, sharing confidential information, spending time together outside of work)	Significant impact on positive emotions at work
Personal growth (being challenged and supported, having role models)	Significant impact on life satisfaction
Having opportunities to help others	Significant impact on more meaningful work

Additional benefits of positive professional relationships may include experiencing a shared interest in a concept, issue, or area of work; a shared sense of purpose; a sense of belonging and solidarity; an atmosphere of camaraderie; and the opportunity to develop a professional identity. Relationships that enable you to not only succeed but also to flourish in your career may be among those things that mark the difference between a "good-enough" job and a great job. The following exercise prompts you to think explicitly about the impact your current work relationships have on you and on your practice.

EXERCISE: RELATIONSHIP JOURNALING

In a journal, take some time to answer the following questions. There are no right or wrong ways to interpret these questions. Let your mind wander.

1. First, thinking of work relationships in general, what do you see as the most valuable benefits of these connections, and why are these valuable? You may consider the benefits discussed earlier, or write about other benefits you have experienced.

2. Which are the most important relationships in your work life, and how would you describe the individuals involved?

3. When, under what conditions, and how, do you interact together?

4. In what ways do you and these individuals invest in these relationships?

Humans are by nature social animals, although to varying degrees. The benefits of significant professional relationships may vary greatly from context to context and from individual to individual.

WHAT: SOCIAL NETWORKS AND SOCIAL CAPITAL

In a social network approach, behavior is enabled or constrained by patterns of interconnected relationships.
—Ferris et al. (2009, p. 1383)

Amir, who works in the information center of a large financial services corporation, can categorize his professional relationships according to how near they fall to the information center itself—the heart of his professional domain. He works most closely with Amy, also a librarian, and the two of them report to a division chief who oversees the library along with two other departments. Because one of Amir's primary roles in the information center is to monitor business, industry, and finance news and to circulate alerts to the corporation's traders, financial analysts, and wealth managers, relationships with these individuals form the next level of closeness. Amir interacts with each of these professionals regularly and has worked hard to get to know them and understand what kinds of information they rely on to complete their work. At the next level are those groups with whom Amir works on projects that cross departmental lines. For instance, he is on a working group with members of the in-house legal team and the organization's compliance officer, Alicia, to review and revise retention, privacy, and copyright policies for the corporation's archives. Because so much of what he does is technology dependent, he is in frequent contact with the cybersecurity team and members of the IT department. Lastly, Amir also strives to maintain an external network with vendors, contacts in other financial services firms, and individuals who are active in an industry association. At each level, he would describe some individual relationships as close and others as more strictly professional. There is Amy, who took him under her wing when he joined the firm and has provided various types of support since. There are a few individuals with whom he collaborates on multiple projects or initiatives, those with whom he socializes a bit, and just one or two who occasionally bring along family members to the backyard picnics hosted by Amir and his husband.

Those who study relationships at work describe a web comprising one's *social network*, where individuals serve as *nodes* connected via *ties* (relationships), and the individual actor who may be under examination—the central figure whose situation is being described—is called the *ego*. As characterized by Granovetter (1973), within a social network, members of close *social cliques* will have very *strong ties* with each other, involving frequent, often emotional interactions, and multiple concurrent relationships. The group of finance professionals working closely with Amir shares multiple strong bonds, related to many different areas of work. Some of them also meet up most afternoons in the lunchroom, and he and one of the analysts, John, decompress over beer and cheese fries at the local pub once in a while. Camila and her fellow collaborators on the high school outreach initiative might also be described as a clique. Through strong, redundant, and overlapping connections, clique members share information quickly and easily and garner support from each other in many ways. According to Coleman (1988), when an individual actor has relationships with actors who also share ties, trust increases as does closer adherence to network norms. In other words, in a social clique as theorized by Granovetter (1973) and others, individuals develop a great deal of confidence in the network itself and come to share practices and approaches to various situations. The traders, wealth managers, and financial analysts in Amir's company all work very closely together, and he has become a key member of their team. Over time, the group has developed clear communication channels and customary practices for sharing new information.

In contrast, *weak ties*—connections that reach beyond one's close circle of colleagues and are characterized by a single type of relationship and less frequent, less intense interactions—are beneficial in a different way, providing access to information or advantages that may be rare within the network. When an ego has individual ties to two or more nodes, but those nodes are not tied to each other, a *structural hole* can be identified between the unconnected nodes, where a tie might otherwise exist (Figure 2.1).

When we think about networking, common sense might dictate that it's best to have as many relationships as possible and that stronger relationships are always better, period. However, Burt (1992) argues for the benefits of a network with sparse and nonredundant connections and a large number of structural holes, which may place the individual in a more powerful position as broker of scarce information and advantage. An ego with a significant number of weak ties and structural holes has greater access to more valuable or strategic information, is well positioned to bargain for resources, and develops high visibility within the network (Burt, 1992). Amir and Alicia share a weak tie. Beyond the few members of the policy task group, they don't share connections with other nodes. Through participation in the policy initiative, Amir is positioned well to provide his supervisor with the kinds of information he garners there, to which his supervisor otherwise wouldn't have access. This is because, within Amir's network, there is a structural hole between his supervisor and the other members of the policy team. It may seem counterintuitive to aim to cultivate weak ties or structural holes, but research supports the idea of these as valuable in their own right.

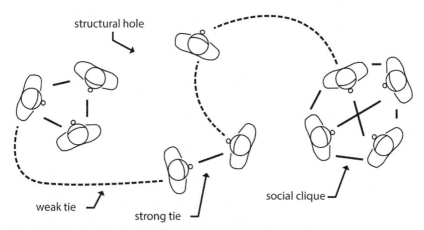

Figure 2.1   Social network diagram.
Source: Adapted from a work in the public domain by Sadi Carnot.

Social capital is conceived of as the value that derives from all of these connections, created through interactions among members—the information, influence, or advantage that can be invested, traded, or consumed by various actors within the network. "Social capital is the goodwill available to individuals or groups. Its source lies in the structure and content of the actor's social relations. Its effects flow from the information, influence, and solidarity it makes available to the actor" (Adler & Kwon, 2002, p. 23). Social capital may include access to information, skill or expertise, material resources, career sponsorship, bargaining power, and so forth. Individual actors within the network invest resources into relationships in the hopes of one day reaping undefined benefits. According to Adler and Kwon (2000), social capital may complement other types of capital or substitute for a particular type of capital that is deficient—for instance, when someone with strong, relevant, and unique relationships has great value, even if they do not have much financial capital. Where does social capital come from? One source of social capital is the network itself, one's membership and interaction in the network, as well as the individual ties between actors, or nodes leave (p. 97). Return on investment (ROI), however, can be unpredictable. Active participation in relationships generally always increases one's social capital, but of course this is dependent on the continued cooperation of both parties to a given relationship (pp. 93–94). Social capital may accrue differently in different network configurations, because of the ways cliques, weak ties, and structural holes function. Thus, for Amir, social capital is generated via the trust and norms generated within his clique—among he and the finance professionals he works with most closely—and via access to valuable information thanks to his weak ties with other individuals in the organization, like Alicia.

Beyond the network itself and its dynamics as source of social capital, circumstances and an individual's outlook and strengths can also impact social capital development. Adler and Kwon (2002) propose a three-part framework of opportunity-motivation-ability as a way to conceptualize under what conditions social capital may be generated. They contend that all three of these elements must be present: *opportunity* in the form of connections or accessibility to nodes, *motivation* of both parties, and some type of *ability* (one's skills, knowledge, experience, resources, and/or influence) that must be valuable or attractive to the other individual. Individuals need to be able to interact with each other in order to form connections, they need to be motivated, and they need to possess something valuable or the promise of something of value that might accrue in the future.

Other factors seen as key to development of social capital are related to how individuals coalesce into groups over time: reciprocity, group norms, and organizational structure. Confidence in the network—the idea that one's investment in a given relationship in the moment will pay off in some future, unspecified way—derives, in part, from a sense of shared responsibility for the well-being of all. Generalized reciprocity "transform[s] individuals from self-seeking and egocentric agents, with little sense of obligation to others, into members of a community with shared interests and a sense of the common good" (Adler & Kwon, 2000, p. 99). Cooperation helps foster development of network norms, which help ensure predictability of behavior. Thus, shared beliefs about the world, assumptions, and expectations enable unambiguous communication, common understanding, and, ultimately, joint action and solidarity (p. 99). Rules, or other institutional structures that impose order, also have an impact on the development and circulation of social capital for a number of reasons. For one thing, the formal network of an organization necessarily helps shape the informal ties that may develop, by providing or constraining opportunities for interaction. Also, the ways individuals perceive the relative transparency, fairness, and responsiveness of an institution—the level of perceived justice or integrity—can impact how social capital develops or fails to do so (p. 100). The building of one's social capital is not only up to the individual but also relies on shared enterprise, consensus, and organizational structure and integrity.

Exercise: Network Mapping

1. Develop a visual diagram of your professional network with you at the center.

2. Begin by adding in all of the people (nodes) with whom you currently share relationships, using solid lines to represent strong ties and dotted lines to represent weak ties. Include relationships that exist within your organization and those that represent network connections you have developed outside of work.

3. To the best of your knowledge, add in lines representing all of the relationships these nodes share with each other.

4. Add nodes and lines to depict any relationships you have observed over time between the individuals in your immediate network and individuals with whom you do not currently share any kind of relationship.

5. Identify the structural holes in this network.

6. Using a new color, draw aspirational nodes and ties—think about how you could garner new strategically placed or high-status contacts or where you might be able to access benefits such as valuable information, resources, or sponsorship. At the same time, remember that a strategically developed network will have a balance of strong ties, weak ties, and structural holes.

Developing a clear picture of your key relationships and of how social capital circulates within your network can help you understand the value in each connection and help you realize the potential value that could come from current or new ways of interacting. It can also provide a good sense of how relationships work for your colleagues, supervisors, or staff.

WHO: TYPES OF SUPPORTIVE WORKING RELATIONSHIPS

Finding your tribe offers more than validation and interaction, important as both of those are. It provides inspiration and provocation to raise the bar on your own achievements.
—Robinson (2009, p. 118)

Workplace and networking relationships are important throughout a professional career, although we tend to focus most keenly on developing and nurturing relationships during those times when we feel most in need of a professional boost—for instance, when we are starting out in a new field, a new workplace, or a new job; when we are taking on a new area of work; when we are hoping to advance; or when we find ourselves suddenly underemployed. "Developmental relationships" is a catchall term often used to describe those professional relationships that emphasize support for career development, such as mentoring, sponsorship, or allyship. Higgins (2000) studied different types of developmental relationships in combination, testing whether these developmental relationships provide more satisfaction when they are solely or primarily focused on career advancement, psychosocial well-being, or both. She determined that high levels of satisfaction were predicted in two specific situations: when an individual has a large number of developmental relationships overall and when an individual has mainly one relationship—with a peer or superior—that includes very high levels of psychosocial support. Based in part on these findings, she theorized a new type of developmental role (to join mentor, sponsor, and ally), that of "friend."

From among those with whom she volunteers on the planning committee for the regional archival association's annual conference, Camila has developed a particularly close relationship with Denise, another archivist who works in the library of a nearby college. The kind of support they exchange is less practical and more psychosocial, less task- or advancement-oriented and more focused on encouragement and inspiration. They bounce around ideas for new projects and serve as each other's sounding board. They keep one another accountable by checking in with each other about goals and progress. Although they don't socialize with each other beyond the committee, each asks after the other's family, celebrating personal as well as professional victories. This relationship might qualify as "friend" in Higgin's conception.

The typology found in Table 2.3 is built on Higgins's work, and it also includes the consideration of colleagues, supervisors, and supervisees.

It may be useful to think about different kinds of relationships according to structure—how vertical or horizontal they are or how the benefits flow among the participants. Supervisor-supervisee relationships typically provide unidimensional task- or role-specific support flowing from one individual to the other, and mentoring and sponsorship are also typically unidimensional. This is not to suggest that the supervisor, mentor, or sponsor doesn't also find these connections gratifying. For example, it is easy to imagine that the best mentor-mentee relationships contribute substantively to "flourishing" for the mentor, as theorized by Colbert, Bono, and Purvanova (2016): this work is meaningful, it contributes to job and life satisfaction, and it may increase the experience of positive emotions at work. In addition, support for new and aspiring professionals is a foundational value for many in the library field, in some cases drummed into us during our master's training, right alongside Ranganathan's *The Five Laws of Library Science* (1931). It feels like part of our mission. There may also be a perception that the protégé, reaping the benefits in the present, will one day be contributing valuable social capital to the network, for the benefit of all.

When Allen (2006) reviewed the research literature on mentors and mentees, she found that mentors are attracted to potential protégés who have a positive track record for job or task performance, show the potential

Table 2.3   Typology of work relationships.

Role	Type of support	Directionality
Mentor/mentee	High career and psychosocial support	Typically from mentor to mentee
Sponsor/protégé	High career support; no psychosocial support	Typically from sponsor to protégé
Friend	High psychosocial support; perhaps no career support	Typically reciprocal
Ally	Low career and psychosocial support; willing to help as needed	May be reciprocal
Colleague	May include career, psychosocial, or task-specific support	Typically reciprocal
Supervisor/supervisee	High role- or task-specific support	Typically from supervisor to supervisee

to achieve, and are adaptable and willing to accept feedback. It's also a good idea to pay attention to the networking behaviors and other traits of potential new connections in the workplace. Some researchers have found that male mentors are likely to provide more direct career development support, while female mentors are likely to provide more psychosocial support to mentees. If you are thinking of reaching out to attract a mentor, you may want to target someone whom you observe generally providing empathy and support in the workplace, someone who has an internal locus of control (sees themselves as in control of their own life), and who exhibits a level of upward ambition. According to Allen (2006), these traits are common among mentors, along with previous experience in a mentoring relationship, either as mentor or mentee.

In contrast to mentorship, the structures of allyship and friendship both suggest a two-way, give-and-take support and may often take place among peers. In addition, the term *collegial* is often used to refer to relationships that are more peer focused, featuring reciprocal career, psychosocial, and/ or task-specific support. Colleagues may work together in the same institution or work together on projects that cross institutional lines, as in the conference planning committee for which Camila and Denise volunteer. Peer relationships, in contrast to supervisory or other more vertical connections, feature what Kram and Isabella (1985) refer to as "mutuality," a more or less equal sharing of responsibility and benefit, which "appears to be critical in helping individuals . . . develop a continuing sense of competence, responsibility, and identity as experts" (p. 117). It may be that working with peers on the planning committee, without the scrutiny of superiors, has enabled Camila's development of such traits. She has been able to take responsibility for specific tasks, take chances, build confidence, and develop a professional persona, without direct oversight from her superiors.

We've discussed a number of different types of professional relationships: supervisor, mentor, colleague, and so forth. But, of course, sometimes these are not so easy to categorize, and roles may overlap—for instance, when a supervisor is also a mentor to their supervisee or, in some circumstances, serves as an ally. In addition to supervising and evaluating Camila, the literary institute's associate director, Michelle, serves as a role model and provides advice about navigating interoffice politics and bureaucratic red tape. This melding of roles exists within the literature about mentoring, where an individual relationship may be described as involving mentoring, sponsorship, friendship, and so forth, under the singular appellation of "mentor." Generically speaking, mentoring is when someone who has accrued a certain level of experience supports an individual with less experience, often someone who is trying to get a job, move up in an organization, or succeed with a complex task or unfamiliar role. These developmental relationships may be organized and supported formally by an institution or organization or informally constituted after one party approaches the other. Sometimes they grow organically with exposure, opportunity, and close collaboration. Sponsorship is when someone with clout puts in a good word for, or positions themselves as a visible support of, an individual seeking advancement or a specific opportunity. Although most common in early or transitional career phases, developmental functions can have a significant positive impact on the recipient at any stage. In some cases, mentors directly support career development through coaching, advising, or helping with certain tasks or projects. Sponsors or mentors may promote an individual's visibility within the organization, backing their candidacy for specific opportunities, or may work to shield their protégé from potentially damaging political maneuvering. Psychosocial support from a mentor, sometimes less direct, may include acting as role model or providing advice, friendship, and acceptance (Kram & Isabella, 1985, p. 111).

Ally and colleague are also roles that frequently overlap. Although allyship has been linked in recent library and information science (LIS) literature with social justice, diversity, and equity work—as it has within other fields (e.g., Amundsen, 2017; Becker, 2017)—in the literature about workplace relationships an ally is typically defined as someone who advocates for you as regards a specific project or career goal. A colleague, in contrast, is someone with whom you collaborate—someone who works with you to attain some sort of shared project goal. An ally is like a sponsor who is also a peer rather than a superior. When you stand up for someone or use your connections to help a peer garner approval for some initiative and so forth, you are acting as an ally. When you collaborate on a project or work on a team, you are maintaining a collegial relationship. As colleagues, you may find yourselves sharing stories about the similar work you do and asking or offering advice. When this activity is sustained and shared among members of a network, you may actually be forming a community of practice (Wenger, 1998).

EXERCISE: ROLES AND TYPES OF SUPPORT

1. Look back at your network map. Review for yourself the identity of each individual node and reflect on your ties to that person.

2. On paper or in an electronic journal, describe each relationship:

   a. What role does the individual play in your work or career? You may consider the roles discussed previously, or write about any different kinds of relationships you have experienced.

b. What type of support do you and the other individual supply and/
or receive?

c. How strong or weak is the tie? Do you connect with that person on
one or on multiple levels?

3. Reviewing these qualities of your current relationships, were there any
surprises? Did anything in particular stand out to you?

Once you have identified the types of supportive relationships you have currently, are there any types of support we've discussed that you haven't received? It may be worthwhile to think about broaching the possibility of building on some of your existing relationships in new ways or cultivating new contacts that could lend such support.

HOW: NETWORKING BEHAVIOR

In this era of boundaryless careers, with individuals making frequent career moves and needing to get up-to-speed quickly, networking is seen as a critical competency.

—de Janasz and Forret (2007, p. 629)

Networking is a collection of behaviors and actions undertaken to build, grow, and maintain a network of relationships that one hopes will ultimately provide career advantages and/or psychosocial support. Forret and Dougherty (2001, 2004) identify five categories of networking behavior: (1) internal visibility within the organization, (2) participating in professional activities, (3) socializing, (4) maintaining external relationships (beyond the organization), and (5) participating in community activities (beyond the workplace). Perhaps it's no surprise that each of these things could be beneficial to your career—they all sound great, right? But which activities provide the biggest payoffs, and in what ways? Examining the effect of these behaviors on career outcomes, such as number of promotions, compensation rate, and one's own perceptions of career success, Forret and Dougherty (2004) found that participation in professional activities and higher visibility within the organization had significant impact, socializing behavior had only marginal positive effect, and maintaining external relationships and participating in community activities had even less impact. The specific types of impact in these findings (on promotions, compensation, and/or perceived success) varied (Table 2.4).

As we might have predicted, each of these types of networking behavior proved to have a positive impact, although to varying degrees and in varying ways. It's worth noting that the individuals included in Forret and

Table 2.4   Networking behaviors and levels of impact. Findings from Forret and Dougherty (2004).

Networking behaviors	Impact on promotions, compensation, perceived career success
Internal visibility (through task assignments, participation on committees, etc.)	Significant impact on promotions, salary, and perceptions of success
Participating in professional activities (through professional organizations, speaking engagements, etc.)	Significant impact on salary and perceptions of success
Socializing (through work functions, athletics, or getting together outside of work, etc.)	Marginal effect on perceived success only
Maintaining external professional relationships (beyond the organization)	Less than marginal impact on all three measures
Participating in community activities (outside of the workplace)	Less than marginal impact on promotions only

Dougherty's (2004) study were all "managerial and professional employees" (p. 419), who had graduated with business school degrees and averaged fifteen years on the job (p. 424). Networking behaviors and benefits may play out very differently among library school graduates or even vary among those who take on different types of roles in different types of libraries.

For the behavior categories we're considering, it's easy to imagine the types of activities involved: taking on special projects or committee assignments, joining a task group for a professional organization, sharing homemade banana bread with coworkers, visiting with colleagues or vendors during conferences, or volunteering at the local animal shelter. Forret and Sullivan (2002) detail a range of potential networking strategies. For example, in addition to socializing with peers, they suggest paying equal attention to those above and below you in the workplace hierarchy (p. 253). Conversations with superiors about their vision and priorities and with those you supervise about their own career development are good investments in social capital. Follow up with individuals you have worked with in the past but haven't heard from in a while, and reach out with a "thank you" to anyone who has helped you. Networking beyond your workplace might involve site visits to colleagues from other libraries. This is not only a way to connect with others, but being on-site can inform and influence your discussions of practice and innovation. It's time now to take stock: What kind of networker are you? And what opportunities can you identify to increase your network advantages?

EXERCISE: NETWORKING BEHAVIORS WORKSHEET

Detail your current networking behaviors in the second column in the following table. Based on your professional context and the connections you may already have, speculate about opportunities for future participation in the third column.

	My current networking behaviors	Opportunities
Internal visibility (task assignments, participation on committees, etc.)		
Participating in professional activities (professional organizations, speaking engagements, etc.)		
Socializing (work functions, athletics, or getting together outside of work, etc.)		
Maintaining external professional relationships (beyond the organization)		
Participating in community activities (outside of the workplace)		

Forret and Dougherty (2001) also studied what types of individuals are most likely to engage in these networking behaviors, determining that an individual's degree of extroversion was the best predictor of participation in four out of the five networking behaviors and that high self-esteem predicted three behaviors. Those with higher socioeconomic backgrounds were more likely to work to maintain external relationships than were others, perhaps unsurprisingly, since prior connections and the financial flexibility to attend conferences and other events probably play a role in one's ability to access these networks. In addition, those who had positive feelings about workplace politics were more likely than others to develop higher visibility within the organization. Again, none of this is really surprising, and while it's true that some of these characteristics are beyond an individual's control or represent tendencies that are difficult to modify, understanding how they may be impacting workplace networks could help you become more proactive. As you look to attract new career contacts, you might try to build strength in, or work to demonstrate your affinity for, any of the positive networking behaviors that resonate with you.

Remember that relationships vary—some involve lending friendship, as well as influence, support, and knowledge, but others are groups of people doing work together who aren't necessarily close, the kind of connections that require a measure of competence but not so much sociability. Camila, our archivist, has always been an extrovert. During her master's program, she was consistently the first to volunteer in class and found easy sociability with fellow students and her instructors alike. Reviewing the list of networking behaviors discussed previously, Camila's colleagues would most likely recognize her as a natural networker. Amir, on the other hand, realizes that he is not such a naturally outgoing guy and has had to work deliberately to cultivate effective networking behaviors and make himself an attractive candidate for support or promotion. He tends to avoid the larger social gatherings among colleagues but values the ties he's made with individuals. One strategy has been putting reminders in his calendar to periodically connect with those contacts whom he hasn't heard from in a while. Everyone gets busy and disappears from radar from time to time, even Amir, but a few informal emails provide an opportunity to catch up on what colleagues have been working on and to share his own news and updates. He likes to attend smaller conferences and symposia and has been able to parlay some presentation experience into higher visibility within the firm. Both Camila and Amir are proactive about building a professional network. They implicitly understand how valuable these relationships can be across the course of their careers, providing support in many ways as well as opportunities to reciprocate. When they function well, work relationships help you get the job done, give you confidence and exposure, and make your professional life more fulfilling.

REFERENCES

Adler, P. S., & Kwon, S.-W. (2000). Social capital: The good, the bad, and the ugly. In E. L. Lesser (Ed.), *Knowledge and social capital: Foundations and applications* (pp. 89–115). Newton, MA: Butterworth-Heinemann.

Adler, P. S., & Kwon, S.-W. (2002). Social capital: Prospects for a new concept. *The Academy of Management Review, 27*(1), 17–40.

Allen, T. D. (2006). Mentoring. In G. A. Callanan & J. H. Greenhaus (Eds.), *Encyclopedia of career development* (Vol. 2, pp. 486–493). Thousand Oaks, CA: SAGE Reference.

Amundsen, J. (2017). Intersections: On allyship. Retrieved from http://www.ala.org/advocacy/intersections-allyship

Becker, J. (2017). Active allyship. *Public Services Quarterly, 13*(1), 27–31.

Burt, R. S. (1992). *Structural holes: The social structure of competition*. Cambridge, MA: Harvard University Press.

Colbert, A. E., Bono, J. E., & Purvanova, R. K. (2016). Flourishing via workplace relationships: Moving beyond instrumental support. *Academy of Management Journal, 59*(4), 1199–1223.

Coleman, J. S. (1988). Social capital in the creation of human capital. *American Journal of Sociology, 94*, S95–S120.

de Janasz, S. C., & Forret, M. L. (2007). Learning the art of networking: A critical skill for enhancing social capital and career success. *Journal of Management Education, 32*(5), 629–650.

Dority, G. K. (2016). *Rethinking information work: A career guide for librarians and other information professionals*. Santa Barbara, CA: Libraries Unlimited.

Ferris, G. R., Liden, R. C., Munyon, T. P., Summers, J. K., Basik, K. J., & Buckley, M. R. (2009). Relationships at work: Toward a multidimensional conceptualization of dyadic work relationships. *Journal of Management, 35*(6), 1379–1403.

Forret, M. L., & Dougherty, T. W. (2001). Correlates of networking behavior for managerial and professional employees. *Group & Organization Management, 26*(3), 283–311.

Forret, M. L., & Dougherty, T. W. (2004). Networking behaviors and career outcomes: Differences for men and women? *Journal of Organizational Behavior, 25*(3), 419–437.

Forret, M. L., & Sullivan, S. E. (2002). A balanced scorecard approach to networking: A guide to successfully navigating career changes. *Organizational Dynamics, 31*(3), 245–258.

Granovetter, M. S. (1973). The strength of weak ties. *American Journal of Sociology, 78*(6), 1360–1380.

Higgins, M. C. (2000). The more, the merrier? Multiple developmental relationships and work satisfaction. *Journal of Management Development, 19*(4), 277–296.

Kay, F. (2009). *How to build successful business relationships*. Stevenage, England: Institution of Engineering and Technology.

Kram, K. E., & Isabella, L. A. (1985). Mentoring alternatives: The role of peer relationships in career development. *Academy of Management Journal, 28*(1), 110–132.

Ranganathan, S. R. (1931). *The five laws of library science*. London, England: Edward Goldston.

Robinson, K. (2009). *The element: How finding your passion changes everything*. London, England: Penguin Books.

Stroebe, W., & Stroebe, M. (1996). The social psychology of social support. In E. T. Higgins & A. W. Kruglanski (Eds.), *Social psychology: Handbook of basic principles* (pp. 597–621). New York, NY: Guilford Press.

Wenger, E. (1998). *Communities of practice: Learning, meaning, and identity*. Cambridge, England: Cambridge University Press.

3

Getting Your Bearings: Understanding Organizational Culture

Any social unit that has some kind of shared history will have evolved a culture, with the strength of that culture dependent on the length of its existence, the stability of the group's membership, and the emotional intensity of the actual historical experiences they have shared.
—Schein (2004, p. 11)

When Sana arrived at the college three years ago to begin her first semester, she made some assumptions about how things got done in the library, based on prior experience at a previous academic library job. This is a perfectly reasonable strategy—bring a frame of reference from past experience and apply it to a new situation. One thing that was different here was obvious: Sana's new colleagues seemed to have quite a bit of latitude to determine where to focus their energy. This was a welcome prospect for her. During that first semester, she spent time thinking about what kinds of projects she might like to take on and how she might want to focus her research, publication, and service efforts. She met with her supervisor, prepared with a list of potential projects, committee assignments, and academic liaison areas, assuming that she would get feedback to point her in a direction aligned with the priorities of the department and the institution.

Instead, her supervisor responded enthusiastically to *all* of the options described. What initiatives did she want to take on? "Those all sound wonderful, and here's a few bits of information about how that work has been approached in the past." Sana's supervisor was wholly supportive but did little to help her prioritize and choose. "Yes," her supervisor continued, "I think your colleague Jane may be working on a project similar to that, but I'm not sure I have the details right." It soon became clear that not only did library faculty at this institution have a lot of professional autonomy when it came to determining their own work but they also seemed to work somewhat in isolation from one another. Not even the library director knew what all of the library professionals were up to! In Sana's previous position, the library director delegated responsibilities to individual librarians not only based on position, expertise, and interest but also based on the strategic plan of the institution and the library. Each professional was like a strategic partner but not a total free agent. The realization of how this process played out differently in her new workplace became an important consideration for Sana. For example, she knew she had to take responsibility for keeping abreast of what each of her colleagues was working on herself and needed to think strategically on her own, as well as consult with her supervisor.

When a librarian is newly hired and is entering the workplace for the first time, it is important that they spend some amount of time observing and listening, in order to "decode" the workplace culture. This is an equally valuable exercise for longtime members of the workplace community wishing to "take stock" of an environment to which they may have grown accustomed. What are the collective values in play? How do people behave and talk in the workplace? Where are the tensions and points of convergence? How do individuals, collaborative partners, and teams get work done? How are decisions really made? How is change introduced and implemented? How do you know when to go with the flow and when and how to resist or stand your ground? Every workplace is different, but awareness of some common challenges, a set of questions to help librarians interpret what they observe around them, and profiles of organizational dynamics in action will support those working to cultivate a professional practice in often complex library environments.

A COMPLEX SYSTEM

Culture is to a group what personality or character is to an individual.
—Schein (2004, p. 8)

Organizational culture is complex on an operational level, serving a number of functions. Culture helps make the work meaningful and purposeful.

It helps make the organization comprehensible to individuals both inside and outside the workplace. It is part of the story we tell about where, how, and why we work. It impacts behavior, both individual and corporate, influencing and explaining what happens on any given workday. Organizational culture also plays a role in structural design and degree of formalization, including development of the policies and procedures that help determine how people are held accountable within the organization. The ways relationships, collaboration, and teamwork operate within a given organization is determined to an extent by how these are viewed and valued within the culture. Finally, organizational culture impacts how each individual's professional identity forms, as it provides a sense of belonging to a larger entity and defines the nature and scope of our commitments.

There are ritual or habitual modes of operation, there are components of organizational culture that are either explicit or implicit, and there are typically both positive and negative effects of culture in any given setting. Organizational culture has been described widely in the literature (e.g., Ballard, 2015; Martin, 2012a; 2012b; Schein, 2004). It is a complex system with many elements, encompassing:

- what members believe and value;
- how they behave;
- rituals, ceremonies, and traditional or habitual ways of getting things done;
- how members understand what's expected of them and what's expected of others; and
- how they understand what's "normal," what's eccentric, and what's unacceptable.

In addition, Ballard (2015) points to the *affective* characteristics of the experience of working in a given setting—things like satisfaction, morale, commitment, and empowerment, as key components of organizational culture (p. 93). All of these core elements exist in a workplace and not in isolation from one another. "Culture somehow implies that rituals, climate, values, and behaviors tie together into a coherent whole," writes Schein (2004). "This patterning or integration is the essence of what we mean by 'culture'" (p. 15). Patterning is one of Schein's five characteristics of culture (pp. 14–15):

1. *Sharing* of values, practices, and so forth
2. A degree of *structural stability*
3. *Depth*, whereby values, norms, and habits are deeply ingrained among members

4. *Breadth*, whereby these deeply held beliefs and understandings influence all aspects of the organization

5. A *patterning* or gestalt or integration of all of these elements into a coherent whole.

As we consider the elements of organizational culture, a picture emerges of a complex system defined by a unique combination of highly detailed assumptions, characteristics, and practices and held together in a pervasive, if somewhat shifting, form.

There is a process called *organizational socialization*, whereby a newcomer, or someone new to a particular position within the organization, learns the associated cultural values and norms, particularly the roles and expectations defined by position or area of responsibility. Sometimes this is explicit. For instance, Sana participated in formal orientation sessions with other new faculty at the college, and she was able to shadow her colleagues at the reference desk during her first few weeks of employment. But sometimes this process happens without our even noticing. Quite often there is a combination of both explicit and implicit socialization. Through participation in meetings, discussions, and various initiatives in the library during the past three years, Sana has developed a very nuanced understanding of how to gain consensus or approval for various measures. She knows, implicitly, when to approach her director one-on-one, when to call upon allies for support, and when to bring an issue to her colleagues as part of a faculty meeting.

One part of organizational socialization, for Ballard (2015), is the development of a "psychological contract," including determining how (and with what effort) we will apply ourselves to work tasks and responsibilities, and figuring out what types of rewards we will expect in return (pp. 73–74). Some of what goes into this bargain is formally negotiated at time of hire, but there is also a body of understanding that develops implicitly, based in part on an individual's experience in other contexts and in part on an evolving understanding of expectations and rewards developed through organizational socialization over time.

A FORCE TO BE RECKONED WITH

The human mind needs cognitive stability; therefore, any challenge or questioning of a basic assumption will release anxiety and defensiveness.
—Schein (2004, p. 32)

Libraries are institutions above all. They are built to last and difficult to change. A few years ago, Joy was exploring ways to revitalize the public areas of her library branch. Fewer and fewer patrons were coming to the library; those who did either came and went quickly—picking up books they'd put on hold through the library's catalog or, if they were inclined to stay awhile and were lucky, finding one of the few vacant armchairs and staking a claim. The physical spaces of the library were neither sufficient nor welcoming. Joy and a few of her younger and more enthusiastic staff formed an exploratory committee and gathered input from staff, patrons in the library, and even from customers at nearby businesses—the very people she hoped would begin to patronize the library after changes were implemented. After collecting a lot of opinions, and considering ideas ranging from simple to complex, Joy and the committee proposed a modest start: the four public services librarians (focused on serving children, youth, adults, and special populations) would collaborate together to plan a number of informal events aimed at drawing people together. Each librarian had previous experience with sponsoring and developing programming for their individual target population. Joy and members of the committee hoped that a new kind of "cross-generational" energy would help the public recognize the library as a social hub for the community. Ultimately, she imagined happier patrons, happier staff, and a significantly altered work culture. As the project began, she was surprised at the strained acceptance the idea received from a couple of her librarians. There was a tension there that she couldn't quite put her finger on. The events went off without a hitch, but the attendance rate was miserable. Somehow the idea never caught on, particularly among the staff. The public service librarians returned to their audience-specific programming roles, where they seemed more content. Even the young and enthusiastic staff members who'd championed the idea all along seemed resigned (or defeated, even). For Joy, the few, muttered "I-told-you-so's" from her librarians stung the most.

Culture plays a key stabilizing role for an organization. Generation by generation, current members impart beliefs, assumptions, and norms to newcomers, which means organizational culture becomes something of a self-perpetuating phenomenon. Habitual ways of doing things become deeply ingrained. This stability (or, as some would say, stagnation) derives from two things: (1) the highly valuable ways organizational cultures provide meaning, purpose, identity, and narrative to members and (2) the tough-to-pin-down nature of their more ephemeral, and somewhat amorphous, characteristics. Culture "points us to phenomena that are below the surface, that are powerful in their impact but invisible and to a considerable degree unconscious" (Schein, 2004, p. 8). If you can't notice it, name it, or describe it, then how can you manage your relationship to culture? How is change possible? Another key reason organizational cultures are so stable may have to do with how humans respond psychologically and emotionally to *dis*-organization. Even temporary upheaval increases anxiety. And predictability—as in, "the way things have always been done around here"—eases that negative affect (Schein, 2004, p. 15). Because members of the organization have developed, and invested in, some of the basic assumptions underpinning their organizational culture, alternate ways of doing things come to seem inconceivable (p. 31). Cultural change, while not impossible, is always difficult, and the extent to which organizations are able to adapt and change overall is determined to a large extent by how difficult it is to change culture.

Successfully navigating culture is a nuanced and sometimes difficult task, requiring excellent intuition, clarity of perception, and persistence. Observation and analysis are primary tools. It is possible that many working professionals, successful in their own right, have adapted well to the cultures of their organizations without ever giving it a second thought. However, efforts invested in this process can benefit both the organization and the individual professional in a number of ways. Martin (2012b) says that "culture can impede or facilitate change, unite or divide members, and cause the library to achieve or fail at its mission. For these reasons, organizational culture is an important concept for librarians to understand." A shared, explicit understanding of what are typically subconscious—or at least unacknowledged—assumptions and modes of operation may be essential for organizational change, collegial relationships, and operation of the library itself. More or less subconsciously *adapting to* the culture of your workplace is valuable, but explicit *understanding* can significantly support development of your professional practice. Knowing how relationships, structures, and workflows function enables productivity, and cultural familiarity may help clarify why some new initiatives fail while others succeed (Ballard, 2015, p. 88). Awareness of cultural dynamics can lessen the anxiety and confusion experienced in response to behavior that seems unusual or eccentric and could help us "better understand the forces acting within us," affecting our own behaviors within and outside of the workplace (Schein, 2004, p. 10). "If we don't understand the operation of these forces, we become victim to them" (p. 3). A nuanced understanding of culture may also specifically support you as a professional who wants to take charge of your own area of responsibilities with confidence and ultimately influence colleagues, leaders, and the organization itself.

DECODING CULTURE

Culture has to be experienced to be truly understood.
—Martin (2012a, p. 348)

Decoding cultural assumptions and behaviors happens naturally, without deliberate attention, as professionals generally acclimate to a new context.

Remember your first day in a new workplace or in a new academic program? Or, imagine the first day of your next job. In what ways did you (or will you) assimilate information to help you tackle your new responsibilities? If you're like Sana, you listened to many people, observed behavior and processes, and asked many questions. Approaching this assimilation deliberately provides awareness of how socialization processes occur and what kinds of knowledge are generated. "We get ideas by watching and listening to others. We determine how accurate those ideas are through our experiences" (Ballard, 2015, p. 71). There will be both visible and implicit phenomena to observe and analyze, and you will find yourself forming hypotheses and testing them repeatedly (p. 96). The following questions will get you started thinking about your organizational culture in a purposeful way.

EXERCISE: BASIC ORGANIZATIONAL CULTURE

In a journal, take some time to answer some of the following questions. These have been developed with the writings of Schein (2004), Stanford (2013), and Ballard (2015) in mind. There are no right or wrong ways to interpret these questions. Let your mind wander.

1. What is expected of me by various individuals? What do they see me accomplishing? How does that differ among supervisors, peers, or subordinates?

2. What about the socialization process itself? What are newcomers asked to learn and through what mechanisms?

3. What seem to be the active assumptions among organizational members? What do they really think about the work, patrons, each other, the organization itself, and the profession?

4. How is the workplace itself functioning as a system?

5. How is space being utilized to get the work done? What types of physical, environmental, status, or value-related considerations may have gone into these decisions?

6. When you look around, how are your colleagues succeeding or failing? How do they earn rewards or advance within the organization? What kinds of things get them into trouble?

7. What are the norms for behavior, dress, communication, and approaches to work, particularly among those with whom you will work most closely?

8. What is the reputation of the organization in the community it serves? In the industry? How important is this to organizational members?

This is an exercise that will get you started thinking about some of the signifiers of organizational culture. When awareness of some of these ideas becomes habitual, you will find yourself tuned-in as your institution and its culture evolve.

Those who have written about organizational culture have developed various models to explain the elements involved. Schein (2004) approaches the subject from the perspective of leadership development; Goffee and Jones (2015) examine what cultural characteristics contribute to an ideal working environment; and, from the reverse perspective, Henry, Eshleman, and Moniz (2018) catalog the problems they perceive through their study of "the dysfunctional library," specifically. In addition, Kendrick (2017) suggests a few signs you might look for to help guard against low morale. It is possible to derive a set of questions from each of these sources, which could be utilized individually or in combination to help you examine the practices in your workplace.

For Schein (2004), organizational culture combines two primary elements: the indistinct, ever-changing atmosphere that surrounds members, developed from the ways we interact together, "and a set of structures, routines, rules and norms that guide and constrain behavior" (p. 1). There are also three levels of culture, representing what is observable, what is espoused, and the assumptions beneath (p. 26) (Table 3.1).

Table 3.1   Questions about organizational culture developed based on the model from Schein (2004).

	Atmospheric	Structural
Observable artifacts	What do you notice about the environment, language, or behavior you see or hear around you?	What formal procedures, technology, services, or products do you find?
Espoused beliefs and values	What myths or stories are told?	What is the stated mission of the organization? How is its structure described, formally? (These principles may be lived or merely aspirational.)
Underlying assumptions	Based on what is observable and the narratives told, how would you characterize core beliefs, *shared or individual* (about the organization, its clientele, its purpose, the nature of work)?	Based on what is observable, declared, or described, how would you characterize core beliefs *of the organization* (about its own nature, purpose, modes of operation)?

Goffee and Jones (2015) provide a model based on the acronym DREAMS, signifying six elements they see as key to a workplace culture that is engineered for worker satisfaction and productivity: Difference, Radical honesty, Extra value, Authenticity, Meaning, and Simple rules. Questions were developed with this model in mind (Table 3.2).

In examining what can go wrong within organizational culture, particularly for libraries, Henry, Eshleman, and Moniz (2018) describe important factors that could indicate dysfunction (pp. 20–31). The way questions are asked can sometimes help determine how they are answered. Since the authors' project was an exploration of *dysfunction*, you may find that the questions developed around this model of culture tip the scale toward the negative, but they also introduce illuminating concepts, such as flexibility, value, and dissent (Table 3.3).

Examining instances of low morale among academic librarians, Kendrick (2017) points to leadership styles and workplace issues that those who have experienced low morale have identified as problematic. Again, some of the concepts surfaced through these questions are valuable, despite the negative paradigm of studying low morale, specifically (Table 3.4).

Taken together, these models cover a lot of ground. Depending on individual context, some may resonate more strongly than others. For example, based on her desire to find her place within a library structure that is

Table 3.2 Questions about organizational culture developed based on the model from Goffee and Jones (2015).

Difference	When it comes to perspectives and habits of mind, does the organization tend to value and encourage difference or conformity?
Radical honesty	When things are happening at the top levels of the organization, at what stage are individual members apprised?
Extra value	In what ways do people feel enriched through their work experiences, or exploited?
Authenticity	How consistent are the organization's identity and mission? If values change, how much do those changes seem to be a matter of deliberate evolution versus fluctuating for no apparent reason?
Meaning	How do individuals view their work on a spectrum from meaningful on one end and alienating or worthless on the other?
Simple rules	Do the policies, procedures, and rules make sense? Or do they seem to present "a miasma of bureaucratic rules [limiting] creativity and effectiveness"? (p. 13)

Table 3.3 Questions about organizational culture developed based on the model from Henry, Eshleman, and Moniz (2018).

Communi-cation	• How well informed do members of the community feel about new ideas and issues?
	• How well matched is mode of communication with preferences of the intended recipients?
Bureaucracy, dictatorship, and management	• What is the balance between set procedures and oversight on one hand, which helps keep everyone accountable, and the flexibility needed for members to adapt and grow?
	• How are supervisory and subordinate roles determined and facilitated?
	• How does delegation happen?
	• How do individual supervisors foster motivation and creativity?
Collaboration and silos	• How do administrators and colleagues value and approach collaboration?
	• Is a siloed structure impacting basic awareness of operations across the organization?
	• Is there duplication of effort or contradictory effort happening?
Word over deed	• Does the organization accomplish what it sets out to do in its mission and goal statements?
	• What is it doing to help move in that direction?
	• Do any individuals seem to be working contrary to the mission or at cross-purposes with each other?
Stress levels	• What kinds of problems are causing stress for individuals?
	• How would they describe their own stress levels?
	• What are the customary ways of dealing with stress?
	• How supportive is the organization as a whole in helping individuals address these issues?
Problematic office politics	• Do individuals or divisions seem to work toward achieving their own narrow agendas, or those of allies, without prioritizing the needs and goals of the organization or its constituents?
	• Are there healthy openness and balanced debate when people or factions disagree?
	• Who are the power players, and who are the disadvantaged?
Diversity	• How much diversity is there among the workforce? The management? The patron base?
	• How much is diversity of assumptions, work styles, or perspectives on librarianship accommodated or encouraged?
	• How often and to what extent is dissent given serious consideration?

Table 3.4   Questions related to leadership and workplace issues, based on concepts from research by Kendrick (2017).

Leadership	• Are leaders in the organization compassionate and flexible with organizational members?
	• To what extent do you observe tolerance for bullying or abuse among members?
	• Do leaders seem absent, ambivalent, negligent, or apathetic?
Workplace issues	• Do you see any signs of understaffing? To what extent does it seem employees are expected to be available at all times or are given unrealistic work schedules?
	• Are there instances where employees seem to be relegated primarily to unchallenging or unfulfilling work?
	• To what extent do you observe colleagues who are struggling with disillusion with the profession, stress, anxiety, work dread, lack of confidence, or increased mistrust of colleagues, leadership, or the institution?

very different from her past experience, Sana might key in most closely to a few of the questions developed in response to Henry, Eshleman, and Moniz (2018) related to accountability, flexibility, different roles, and delegation. Joy, on the other hand, who is interested in managing change in her public library branch, might choose to focus on questions that help her examine individual and shared myths or beliefs and the ways professional and support staff balance their own needs, interests, and priorities with those of the organization.

EXERCISE: FOCUSING ON WHAT MATTERS

With your specific work context in mind, determine the areas of organizational culture that are of most immediate interest to you.

1. Select a number of questions from the models discussed previously, addressing issues related to your areas of interest, and respond to those questions in your journal.

2. Based on your responses, what new questions come to mind?

3. What will you examine (or observe) to investigate further? Who will you talk to, and how will you broach the subject with them?

4. Finally, we know that purposeful organizational change is difficult, but that doesn't mean that culture isn't constantly shifting. What are some strategies for maintaining your awareness of the evolving organizational culture in your workplace?

Since each context is different and each professional comes to an institution or new position with a unique set of needs and expectations, selecting the most relevant questions for your investigation of organizational culture and tailoring your approach will help you focus on what's most significant for your professional practice.

EMPOWERMENT AND ENGAGEMENT

For collaboration to work, the library organization must embrace the team concept and empower its employees to make decisions.
—Henry, Eshleman, and Moniz (2018, p. 129)

To empower someone gives them the control—or power—to do something, and *empowerment* is the process of becoming stronger and more confident, particularly in relation to your own self-determination. McClelland (1970) introduced the concept of the two "faces" of power: one being the personal, dominant-submissive model (i.e., I win, you lose) and the other being social, characterized by a "concern for group goals, for finding those goals that will move [individuals], for helping the group to formulate them, for taking some initiative in providing members of the group with the means of achieving such goals, and for giving group members the feeling of strength and competence they need to work hard for such goals" (p. 41). The personal face of power—perhaps the one we are most familiar with when we think about power relationships—runs the risk of creating a culture of aggression and domination, whereas a social empowerment model theoretically makes individuals (e.g., staff, colleagues, students, team members) feel more powerful and able to accomplish things on their own (p. 41). Harvey and Drolet (2004) posit that the more people who have power, from a variety of sources, the more stable and healthy an organization will be (p. 167). So, what does an empowered workplace look like?

EXERCISE: ORGANIZATIONAL EMPOWERMENT ASSESSMENT

(Adapted from Harvey and Drolet [2004, pp. 168–180])

In a journal, respond to the following prompts about your general work situation:

1. Do you and your colleagues feel that the *tasks and projects* you are working on are important? In what ways are these tasks significant, and for whom? Are there any areas of work that are less than satisfying in this way?

2. How much *professional discretion* do you and your colleagues have in determining the tasks that you will take on and how you will approach the work? Is this true across the board or only in certain areas of responsibility?

3. Are you and your colleagues provided with the *resources* needed to accomplish your work? What types of resources is your organization good at providing, and in what areas does it fall short?

4. How would you rate the level of encouragement you receive for *working together collaboratively*? Are there any areas of work where you would say your organization is resistant to a teamwork approach?

5. Do you and your colleagues feel you are given appropriate *praise and recognition* for the work you accomplish on behalf of the organization? Are there areas of work that you feel do not receive the requisite positive response?

6. To what degree are you and your colleagues encouraged and supported in *improving and developing new skills*? Can you identify any sources of resistance to providing this type of support?

7. To what degree do you and your colleagues feel *responsible for*, and *in control of*, your own future within the organization? Are there any elements of this that are beyond your control?

8. Do you and your colleagues work in an environment that allows for and encourages individuals to develop and implement *innovative approaches*? To what degree are organizational leaders open to surprise over regimented routine and order?

Empowerment of individuals within the organization supports the library's ability to serve its constituency, as well as its capacity to evolve. Henry, Eshleman, and Moniz (2018) argue that a healthy and thriving library culture not only revolves around service and a desire to help others but also includes appreciation for a love of learning and the ability to embrace change and adaptability (pp. 18–19). By empowering us to make decisions on our own, and supporting our efforts to influence organizational practice or promote change and progress, an organization's leaders provide a sense worth, a sense of belonging, a sense of ownership, a sense of competency, and a sense of trust. These are all key factors in creating and maintaining a positive and dynamic organizational culture, which, in turn, leads to more motivated and engaged employees.

Engagement with one's work is critical to one's professional satisfaction as well as to the success of the organization itself. When someone is fully engaged with what they do on a daily basis, they are more able to readily and enthusiastically contribute their skills, complete their work, collaborate with others, take on new challenges, and take pride in themselves and their institution's mission. The Gallup organization (2017), in a report covering its extensive employee engagement research, describes an engaged workplace as one where "employees are highly involved in and enthusiastic about their work and workplace. They are psychological 'owners,' drive performance and innovation, and move the organization forward" (p. 63). The Q^{12} Survey includes questions related to four areas of employee development needs: basic, individual, teamwork, and personal growth (p. 62).

EXERCISE: HOW ENGAGED ARE YOU?

(Adapted from a selection of the Q^{12} Survey questions [Gallup, 2017, p. 63])

In a journal, respond to the following prompts:

1. How confident are you that you know what's expected of you in your current position? Are there areas of work where expectations are less clear than in others?

2. Which of your responsibilities would qualify as some of the things you do best? Are you afforded the opportunity to engage in some of these tasks every day?

3. To what degree do you feel your opinions matter in the workplace? How is this value communicated? What impact does your opinion seem to have?

4. To what degree do you feel that your supervisor, or someone else at work, cares about you as a person? How is this communicated?

5. Would you say that you have a "best friend" at work? If so, how does that relationship play into the work you do, individually and together?

Your responses to these questions, which get at how you feel about the work you do, your institution, your supervisors and colleagues, and the ways you engage with each other in the workplace, can help you understand how organizational culture impacts your level of satisfaction and how it may also be impacting the way you practice professionally.

With a solid understanding of the dynamics of organizational culture in her library, and armed with a plan for maintaining awareness, Sana will be better able to negotiate day-to-day responsibilities, build strategic relationships, and determine how best to define and focus her professional practice. Applying an organizational culture perspective could help Joy understand what motivates resistance to change among staff and patrons and help her determine some strategies for making her branch library into a more engaged, empowered, and collaborative workplace. Information professionals find their way within new organizations all the time, and institutional change does happen, with or without an explicit focus on workplace culture. But one's ability to effectively harness a solid understanding of the ins and outs of organizational structures and dynamics can be a strategic advantage when it comes to career advancement and professional satisfaction and could have a favorable influence on workplace culture as well.

REFERENCES

Ballard, J. (2015). *Decoding the workplace: 50 keys to understanding people in organizations.* Santa Barbara, CA: Praeger.

Gallup. (2017). *State of the American workplace.* Retrieved from https://www.gallup.com/workplace/238085/state-american-workplace-report-2017.aspx

Goffee, R., & Jones, G. (2015). *Why should anyone work here? What it takes to create an authentic organization.* Boston, MA: Harvard Business Review Press.

Harvey, T. R., & Drolet, B. (2004). *Building teams, building people: Expanding the fifth resource.* Lanham, MD: Scarecrow Education.

Henry, J., Eshleman, J., & Moniz, R. (2018). *The dysfunctional library: Challenges and solutions to workplace relationships.* Chicago, IL: ALA Editions.

Kendrick, K. D. (2017). The low morale experience of academic librarians: A phenomenological study. *Journal of Library Administration, 57*(8), 846–878.

Martin, J. (2012a). Symbols, sagas, rites, and rituals: An overview of organizational culture in libraries. *College & Research Libraries News, 73*(6), 348–349.

Martin, J. (2012b). "That's how we do things around here": Organizational culture (and change) in libraries. Retrieved from http://www.inthelibrarywiththeleadpipe.org/2012/thats-how-we-do-things-around-here/

McClelland, D. (1970). The two faces of power. *Journal of International Affairs, 24*(1): 29–47.

Schein, E. H. (2004). *Organizational culture and leadership.* San Francisco, CA: Jossey-Bass.

Stanford, N. (2013). *Organizational health: An integrated approach to building optimum performance.* London, England: Kogan Page.

4

The Choices We Make: Creating Habits for Professional Growth

Habits are powerful factors in our lives. Because they are consistent, often unconscious patterns, they constantly, daily, express our character and produce our effectiveness.

—Covey (1990, p. 46)

Before she took up her current position, and right after library school, Sana worked as a serials librarian at a suburban community college. It was exciting at first. To be honest, there was a lot to love about the job: working with librarians and faculty to identify the best disciplinary resources, evaluating cost-per-use metrics, establishing productive relationships with vendors, and troubleshooting access issues. She settled into the routines of the job and flourished. But over time, evolution took over—evolution of libraries, of users, of serials themselves. In the gradual diversification of her responsibilities to include more public service, project management, and cross-campus collaboration, Sana found that the *habits* and *routines* she had successfully managed for several years were no longer serving her best interests. She was bored with certain parts of her job and overwhelmed by some of her new responsibilities, which led to a lack of focus and a loss of energy. She was still devoted to the institution, loved working with her colleagues and supporting the faculty and students, and enjoyed learning new

57

things, but she knew that she wasn't meeting the expectations of her director and knew that her productivity was increasingly falling short.

The irregularity of our roles and the ever-changing nature of our profession can be a draw for those who crave variety and enjoy learning new things. Librarianship, thankfully, is rarely boring, and library professionals rarely spend their days doing the same tasks with the same routines over and over again. Our daily responsibilities vary greatly by type of institution, job role, community of library users, and personal and professional backgrounds and motivations. The work of an academic serials librarian is very different from that of a children's librarian in a public library setting, or a corporate law librarian, or a medical information specialist. But all of our roles are constantly being redefined and reimagined so that we can keep up with changing technologies, workflows, and patron/client expectations. No matter what role we are in—or hope to be in—at some point we will be simultaneously pulled in many different directions, making it difficult to prioritize one thing at a time, to make decisions, and to get out of our heads in order to focus and move forward with the next goal, project, position, or achievement.

The ability to do certain things automatically, without explicit thinking or planning, allows us to get through our days—and our to-do lists—with more ease. We are better able to prioritize and can spend greater time and effort on the most important issues and tasks. We are better able to focus on learning or systematizing new areas of responsibility, because accomplishing certain other tasks has become routine or habitual. In a way, the habits we develop define our experience and make us who we are. For Covey, author of the bestselling book, *The 7 Habits of Highly Effective People* (1990), life isn't something that just happens to us but is actually constructed *by us*, in part through the habits we cultivate. These are the things that we do regularly, acquired through repetition and over time. They may be intentional or accidental and can become second nature—an involuntary reflex or a subconscious reaction to certain stimuli or cues. Managed well, our habits and routines can help us hone our skills, create structure and focus around specific goals or tasks, and streamline our decision-making processes. This chapter will focus on the good habits—how to develop and use them fruitfully and creatively to get what we want out of our careers and, ultimately, to create an approach to work that is both productive and healthy. Managing habits can mean a variety of different things: cultivating specific habits for productivity, focus, and time management; getting clued in to our "habits of mind"; and developing strategies for habit maintenance and long-term success.

CLEARING THE DECKS

> *The more routine a behavior becomes, the less we are aware of it. . . . This loss of surveillance not only can interfere with our daily functioning, it also can allow bad habits to creep up on us.*
>
> —Graybiel and Smith (2014, p. 40)

There is a fine line between too much automation, which can result in boredom or robotic complacency, and too little, which can make us feel overwhelmed by details. Finding the right balance and taking control of our daily habits and routines are key. Casting around to identify a way to reinvigorate and reanimate her work, Sana decided to focus on habits and routines—reviewing old, reliable habits to see if they'd gone stale; revision or replacement of some; and development of new, productive routines to help her meet new challenges. Habits can help us accomplish goals and achieve success in various areas of our lives, but only if they are applied productively. Taking stock of our current habits and evaluating their usefulness is a good first step. Certain routines may have become so automated that we find ourselves bored, or "checked out," and not really present in our work. Or things that worked well years ago may have become counterproductive as contexts and situations have changed. Sana used the following checklist exercise to evaluate and adjust her habitual approaches to day-to-day responsibilities. You could also repeat this process for project-specific habits, job-searching habits, promotion/tenure habits, or work-life balance or personal habits.

EXERCISE: HABITS CHECKLIST

1. Use the following format to create a table or spreadsheet that describes current habits, expectations for each, and when during the typical week these come into play. Simply replace Sana's habits in the following example with your own.

Habit	Goal/ expectation	Mon	Tue	Wed	Thurs	Fri
Read new emails, respond to urgent ones, and categorize/archive/delete others	30 minutes; daily	X	X	X	X	X
Talk to staff members about their work/projects	15 minutes; 3× week	X		X		X
Write and/or research	30 minutes; 3× week	X		X	X	
Read/peruse current issues of library journals	15 minutes; 3× week	X	X			X
Evaluate reference questions and search queries	30 minutes; 2× week		X		X	
Meet with supervisor about current and new projects	60 minutes; 1× week				X	

2. Review these data, considering what purposes each habit serves, whether they reflect accurate estimates of time or effort, or, at the other end of the spectrum, oversimplify tasks and mask important subtleties.

3. For each habit, consider your goals/expectations and schedule. Are there adjustments that would be beneficial?

4. Finally, are there additional areas (e.g., professional development, community service, outreach) that could benefit from habitual approaches that haven't yet been implemented?

If your answer to the question, "how's work going?" involves feeling somehow "checked out," overwhelmed, or both, you might want to hit the pause button and take time to assess the current habits and rituals of your job. The added benefit of clearing the decks in this manner is an increased sense of autonomy and control of your professional life.

HABITS FOR FOCUS, TIME MANAGEMENT, AND PRODUCTIVITY

A growing body of scientific research shows one of jugglers' favorite timesaving techniques, multitasking, can actually make you less efficient and, well, stupider. Trying to do two or three things at once or in quick succession can take longer overall than doing them one at a time, and may leave you with reduced brainpower to perform each task.
—Shellenbarger (2003, p. D1)

In the fast-paced world of twenty-first-century libraries, the ability to focus on what's most important or most urgent is the key to managing workflows and productivity. Becoming overwhelmed and paralyzed by details and deadlines of the many, many tasks on our plate is one potential consequence of a very busy work life. If we spend too much time worrying about all the things we need to do, we may never get around to actually doing them. You want to keep all those balls in the air but somehow manage them. Allen, in *Getting Things Done: The Art of Stress-Free Productivity* (2001), emphasizes the importance of capturing all the things that need to get done—now or later, big or little—so you don't lose them, putting them into a logical and trusted system outside of your brain and then disciplining yourself to make deliberate decisions to plan and accomplish your priorities (p. 3). By getting these things out of our heads, and organizing and processing them, we can stop trying to keep track of everything all at once. We gain focus for increased productivity. Camila, whose archival job involves many different types of responsibilities, simultaneous supervision of multiple projects, strategic planning for her department, maintenance of a complex network of relationships, and administrative tasks—in other words, a lot of responsibility involving a lot of detail—has taken up Allen's method and adapted it to her particular situation. Allen describes a five-stage approach: (1) collect, (2) process, (3) organize, (4) review, and (5) do (p. 24). Each Monday morning Camila takes a seat in the staff breakroom and opens a notebook, which she likes to refer to as her habit journal.

Exercise: Five Steps to Getting Things Done

(Adapted from Allen [2001])

Follow the next steps, substituting the specifics of your job for the examples from Camila's responsibilities.

Collect	On one page of your journal, write down everything you can think of that needs to get done, and anything that's on your mind or keeping you up at night—in no particular order. Include notes from past weeks for continuing projects or issues.	**Example—from Camila:** *Hiring a project archivist, checking in with a curator regarding a new initiative, preparing for a meeting with her director, submitting a new grant proposal, reorganizing her office, cleaning out her inbox, requesting pricing and trials for digital repository platforms, and revising departmental goals for the upcoming fiscal year.*
Process	Create a page for each project or issue. Transfer any outstanding items from the previous week's notes and jot down any new information or ideas—again, in no particular order.	**Example—hiring a project archivist:** • *Job description—run by Nancy* • *HR about salary schedule, timeline* • *Review grant project description* • *Qualifications: subject expertise over experience?* • *List of where to advertise* • *Reserve a room* • *For the committee—Joan? David? Susan?*
Orga-nize	For each project, consider level of importance and urgency. Set priorities for action today, this week, and/or this month. Track tasks with important deadlines in a calendar.	**Example—hiring a project archivist:** ***Today:*** *HR-salary/timeline, review grant, write description* ***Tomorrow:*** *Nancy-description* ***Next week:*** *advertise* ***By June 1:*** *schedule interviews*

Review	Each day of the week, review to prioritize tasks for the day. What is the *next action* for each project?	Example—Camila's to-dos for today, in order of importance: • *HR-salary/timeline, review grant, write description* • *Send nudge email to supervisor* • *Find and review notes from last week's BB meeting; send agenda*
Do	Jump right in! Focus on those next actions.	

This routine sets up the structure for Camila's day and week and helps her clear her mind of the not-so-important details, making room for all the new snags or issues that will inevitably arise.

Sorting is another strategy for productivity that can be cultivated as a habit or routine. This is especially useful for taming an overflowing email inbox, tidying a desk or office, and so forth. In a 1954 speech, Dwight D. Eisenhower talked about problem solving and priorities: "I have two kinds of problems," he said, "the urgent and the important. The urgent are not important, and the important are never urgent" (as cited in Clark & Sousa, 2018). This concept was taken up by proponents of what is now called the "Eisenhower matrix" or the "Eisenhower box." Colan and Davis-Colan, in their book *Stick with It: Mastering the Art of Adherence* (2013), outline a process based on the Eisenhower matrix, called "The 4Ds" (pp. 56–58) (Figure 4.1). It is rumored that Eisenhower himself used this method (p. 57).

EXERCISE: THE EISENHOWER MATRIX

1. Sort all of the tasks and responsibilities and worries that you can think of related to your work using an Eisenhower box (Figure 4.1) in your journal.

2. Take action using the 4Ds—depending on urgency/importance:

   - **Do It (Urgent/Important):** If the action really needs to be done by you, and can be done quickly (in less than two minutes), then do it now.

   - **Defer It (Not Urgent/Important):** If you are the right person for the job but it can't or doesn't need to happen right now, then defer it until later. Put it in a "next action" list and on your calendar as a reminder.

- **Delegate It (Urgent/Unimportant):** If it needs to get done, but it isn't your responsibility, or if someone else can do it sooner, then delegate it.
- **Dump It (Not Urgent/Unimportant):** If it doesn't matter and doesn't need to be acted on now, delete it. Get it out of your head.

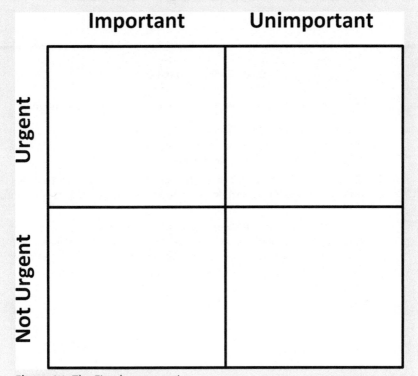

Figure 4.1 The Eisenhower matrix.

In Camila's case, for hiring a new project archivist—*do it:* write/review job description and send for approval; *defer it:* create an interview schedule; *delegate it:* book rooms and make lunch reservations; *dump it:* go through old applications for potential candidates. Common sense tells us that focusing on what's most important requires that we determine which elements are not so important (or not so urgent) and set those aside. Allen's "Getting Things Done" (GTD) approach helps make sure you don't ultimately lose track of anything while you focus on what's next, and the Eisenhower matrix method helps you determine what to prioritize, put off, delegate, or ditch.

If your work frequently involves decision-making related to specific projects or goals, mind mapping may be a useful and creative habit to develop for brainstorming and bringing into focus potential choices or actions. A mind map is basically a visual representation of related information or ideas (Figure 4.2). It is something tangible and customizable, which can help you perceive multiple dimensions of a complex subject, visualize options for decision-making very clearly, and determine what needs to be done next. Mind mapping is a particularly great strategy for visual thinkers.

EXERCISE: MIND MAPPING

Using pen and paper, or a mind-mapping app or tool, create a mind map.

1. Put your main topic/project/focus/task in the center.

2. Building outward, represent related elements or subtasks, drawing connections to show how they are related.

3. Step back and take a look at the big picture—the further out you get from the center, the more hidden elements/ideas/opportunities you can expose.

4. Ask yourself questions to determine how to focus on the information at hand, such as: Where do decisions need to be made? What are the key priorities? What are the next tasks related to each area of work? Who should do them? What resources are needed?

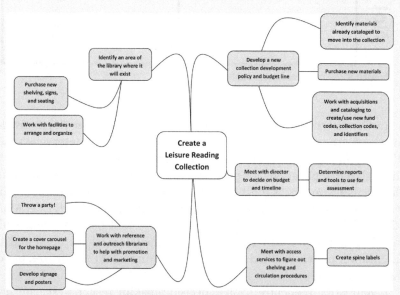

Figure 4.2   Mind map for a leisure reading project, created with MindMup 2 (https://app.mindmup.com/).

In their book, *Creative Confidence*, Kelley and Kelley (2013) promote the importance of prototyping new ideas, action, and intentional practice to unlock one's creative potential. "Actively engaging in exercises that foster divergent or unconventional thinking can encourage the generation of ideas," they write. In their view, mind mapping, in particular, can "help you chart the recesses of your mind surrounding one central idea" (p. 212). Mind maps can spur brainstorming and creativity and reveal decision-making options, new opportunities and relationships, and potential obstacles and consequences. They are also great tools for collaboration and group work and are useful for generating feedback and input from project stakeholders.

One highly valuable area of librarians' work that can get easily sidelined when time is tight is reading and writing. One's professional practice is built on expertise and a body of knowledge, which continually evolve over the course of a career. What's happening "in the field" informs our daily practice in many ways. As a faculty member working toward tenure, Sana is expected to participate in ongoing research and publication, but library professionals of all stripes keep current by reviewing trade and scholarly articles, and some engage in writing about librarianship simply because they love to do it. For all of us, the need for effective written communication—formal or informal—is ubiquitous. And yet, these activities often get shoved to the sidelines—on our radar but easily set aside until the time when daily interruptions and emergencies subside (which we know is never!). How can we formulate and follow good habits around research and writing when there are so many urgent daily tasks looming and interruptions are the norm? "Saying you can't write because of writer's block is merely saying that you can't write because you aren't writing. It's trivial," writes Silvia, author of *How to Write a Lot* (2009), and an expert of sorts on getting past common obstacles to writing. "The cure for writer's block—if you can cure a specious affliction—is writing" (p. 46). Setting up conditions for regular research and writing may require effort, but there are multiple strategies for making the practice habitual. Which of these will prove most productive will depend on the individual.

EXERCISE: DEVELOPING WRITING HABITS

Set-aside time	Schedule uninterrupted time to read, research, and write. Start with thirty minutes until you figure out what duration works best for you. Close your door, or move to a quiet place where you won't be interrupted. Turn off your phone, close your social media accounts, and silence your notifications. Set a timer, if it helps. Make this part of your regular routine and let others know, so they expect it and can help keep you accountable.

Goal setting	Set concrete goals for yourself, such as revise a draft, make an outline, add references, or write X number of words per day. Get in the habit of setting a new goal whenever you've completed the current one, and mark it on your calendar if it's something you know you'll need to pick up after a few days off.
Accountability partners	Find an accountability partner. This person can be someone you are collaborating with, or a colleague or friend, who can check in with you on a regular basis and ask you about your writing and research. If you know you need to report on your progress, then you'll be more motivated to get something done.
Band together	Join or create a research and writing group that meets with some regularity. When you belong to a community of like-minded people, you have an automatic support group and a place to share, ask questions, and encourage one another to keep at it.
External deadlines	Seek out calls for papers/chapters/presentations, and submit your proposals. If you get accepted, then you'll have plenty of motivation (and a hard deadline) to get things done.
"Third place"	Find a writing space that works for you—perhaps one that is not at home or in your office. This alternative space will serve as your "third place," a space with fewer routine distractions (Oldenburg, 1989).
Feel-good space	Create a soothing work space, and incorporate that as part of your habitual practice. If your desk and office are cluttered and unorganized or piled high with projects and work that needs attention, it will be difficult to focus on anything other than what you see in front of you. Declutter, organize, and incorporate things that can help you to focus—better lighting, plants, speakers, aromatherapy, journals, notepads, photos, and so forth.
Reward yourself	Find appropriate ways to reward yourself when you've reached a goal. You deserve it!

If you have colleagues or role models who seem somehow able to juggle research and writing with full careers and hectic daily work lives, ask what strategies they employ and in what combinations. Every writer is different. The key is to find what works best to keep *you* on track and to keep you accountable—to discover and maintain habits that will keep you motivated, energized, productive, and satisfied in your professional life.

MINDSETS AND HABITS OF MIND

Our subconscious programming—developed through our youth and on into adulthood—plays a huge role in how we survive or thrive at work.
—Saunders (2018, p. B5)

In considering habits, we've been focusing a lot on the mind—clearing it, focusing it, mapping it, and so forth. Our minds actually play a huge role in time management and in determining our capacities to change—including our capacities to alter our habits at will. According to Dweck (2006), individuals who believe that "who they are" is set in stone will continually and subconsciously strive to fit a preconceived profile in terms of intelligence, character, morality, personality, and so forth. They seek to match a stable self-image—in other words, they have a *fixed mindset* and believe that change is impossible. And those who see their personal or professional selves as cultivated through effort, and believe that people can change and grow throughout their lives or careers, have a *growth mindset* (pp. 6–7). Individuals in the latter category tend to embrace lifelong learning, continually seek out new knowledge and experience, and have a positive outlook when challenged by adversity or change. Growth-mindset professionals may be more adept at taking on new responsibilities and looking for new ways to approach their work and may be better able to develop and maintain positive habits that could help them achieve their goals. In contrast, those with fixed mindsets might respond with fear to new challenges, not wanting to invest effort or take on the risk of doing something new—a fear of failure. They tend to believe that talent is everything, something you're born with (or not), and that potential, too, is stable and can be measured. So why make the effort if it turns out you are one of those people with neither talent nor potential? Thinking in a certain way about yourself and your potential—your mindset—is habitual, itself.

Exercise: What's Your Mindset?

(Adapted from Dweck [2006, pp. 12–14])

Of the following statements, which most accurately describes what you think about people's intelligence?

1. Someone's intelligence is something they're born with, and it can't be changed very much.
2. Anyone can learn new things, but you can't really change how intelligent you are.

3. No matter how much intelligence a person has, they could always change it quite a bit if they wanted to.
4. You can always substantially change how intelligent you are.

Statements 1 and 2 represent the *fixed* mindset, and statements 3 and 4 represent the *growth* mindset. Dweck points out that you can swap out the word *intelligence* and substitute other abilities such as "artistic talent," "sports ability," or "business skill"—basically your mindset determines your approach to growth and adaptability (or lack thereof) in all areas of endeavor.

If you fall closer to the fixed-mindset end of the spectrum, there's no need to despair. According to Dweck (2014), we all fall prey to at least a little bit of fixed-mindset thinking, but we can change that by tuning in "to hear that fixed-mindset voice when it speaks to us" (telling us that we can't do any better) and by learning to "talk back" with a growth-mindset voice (I think I can, I think I can, I know I can, I know I can! [Piper, Mateu, & Retan, 1930])—until we figure out that we have a choice (p. 15). Ultimately, Dweck proposes that anyone can change their mindset as long as they recognize the problems a fixed mindset can cause and put in the effort to cultivate growth-mindset thinking as a habit.

Our professional success may also be impacted by the way we think about, or feel about, our work. Saunders (2018) talks about "attachment style," referring to the ways individuals psychologically "attach" differently to tasks, projects, or work in general. We may know perfectly well how to manage our time and complete our tasks, but at times, a primal urge to do the opposite takes over and sabotages our best intentions (p. B5). Addressing issues that arise due to attachment style, and understanding and confronting these primal urges, may involve developing some new habitual responses or strategies.

EXERCISE: ATTACHMENT STYLE

(Adapted from Saunders [2018])

Review the following descriptions to determine which attachment style(s) may be impacting your work, and consider ways to build new habitual responses that incorporate some of the potential actions listed.

Attachment style	Characteristics	Actions
Anxious preoccupied	• Afraid others think poorly of you • Fearfully on the lookout for problems • Afraid to say "no"	• Calming self-talk (don't panic—wait and see) • Peer support/reassurance • Work-life boundaries (e.g., no checking email from home)
Fearful avoidant	• Sees trouble where there may be none • Automatic response is to avoid/procrastinate	• Calming self-talk • Peer support/reassurance • Initiate "gentle action" by setting small goals until you stop feeling so "stuck"
Dismissive avoidant	• Frustrated by colleagues who seem to operate with priorities that differ or conflict with your own • Taking on more than your share of work so that it will be done "properly"	• Recognize your own fallibility and your responsibility for helping to establish harmony • Pause to really hear others' ideas, and consider their viability before making a counter proposal
Secure	• Capable, confident, and productive • Managing tasks and time well, maintaining healthy work-life boundaries, and knowing when to ask for help and when to say "no"	• Avoid complacency—regularly solicit feedback and input • Reach out to colleagues if you sense that anything is "off"

Just as using growth-mindset self-talk routinely may help in the transition from a fixed mindset, changing the ways you respond to situations and triggers in the workplace, and making those new strategies habitual, could go a long way toward alleviating the negative impacts of counterproductive attachment styles.

Beyond employing discipline and practice to address mindset and psychological states of attachment, researchers have found that certain habitual ways of thinking can support learning and best practices. Costa and Kallick (2000) suggest that what they term "habits of mind" can help individuals respond thoughtfully and with intelligence when new or challenging situations arise. These researchers were studying K–12 education, but the habitual ways of thinking and responding they describe can have a positive impact on professional success as well.

EXERCISE: HABITS OF MIND WORKSHEET

(Descriptions adapted from Costa and Kallick [2000, pp. 22–38])

Where, in your own work, do you see opportunities for practicing and solidifying these positive habits of mind?

Habit of mind	Actions	Opportunities to develop in your own work
Persisting	• See challenges as problems to be solved. • Draw on a range of strategies for trial-and-error process. • Be comfortable with ambiguity, and take the time needed to get to the goal.	
Managing impulsivity	• Pause before diving in to consider various perspectives and solutions. • Respond thoughtfully and deliberately. • Use *informed* trial-and-error.	
Listening with empathy and understanding	• Listen; read emotions, body language, and subtext. • Don't interrupt or rehearse your response. • Be able to paraphrase; ask for clarification; give examples.	
Thinking flexibly	• Habitually consider alternative points of view, beliefs, and options. • Be open to new information or ideas in problem solving.	
Thinking about thinking (metacognition)	• Be aware of steps in the problem-solving process. • Plan the process, reflect on how your thinking changes, and evaluate progress.	

Habit of mind	Actions	Opportunities to develop in your own work
Striving for accuracy	• Review the products of your thinking and action. • Set and revise standards.	
Questioning and posing problems	• Seek out problems to solve. • See discrepancies or gaps in knowledge as opportunities.	
Applying past knowledge to new situations	• Habitually consider how current situations or problems are analogous to past experiences.	
Thinking and communicating with clarity and precision	• Use the process of language refinement to clarify both thought and communication.	
Gathering data through all senses	• Pay attention to mental images and spatial reasoning. • Use role playing and hands-on experimentation.	
Creating, imagining, and innovating	• Find opportunities for intrinsic motivation. • Juggle alternative perspectives and solutions. • Use analogous thinking, backward thinking, role playing, and risk taking.	
Responding with wonderment and awe	• Seek out problems, puzzles, and challenges. • View thinking not as hard work but as a reward itself	
Taking responsible risks	• View challenges as opportunities but also think first, and then act. • Be comfortable with uncertainty. • Habitually consider how limits might be tested.	
Finding humor	• Cultivate humor as a boost for higher-level thinking (anticipation, seeking novel relationships, analogous thinking). • Be able to laugh at yourself and your own situation.	

Habit of mind	Actions	Opportunities to develop in your own work
Thinking interdependently	• Think and act socially. • Develop cooperative problem-solving skills. • Develop sensitivity to others' feelings and perspectives.	
Remaining open to continuous learning	• Develop a "growth mindset" (see earlier; Dweck [2006]). • View challenges with anticipation, not fear or defensiveness.	

Taking up new habits, be they behavioral or cognitive, takes more than self-awareness and opportunity. "Habits are formed when the brain takes a shortcut and stops actively thinking about the decision being made" (Colan & Davis-Colan, 2013, p. 32). Getting to that stage is the challenge.

MAKING IT STICK

It takes skill to bring something you've imagined into the world: to use words to create believable lives, to select the colors and textures of paint to represent a haystack at sunset, to combine ingredients to make a flavorful dish. No one is born with that skill. It is developed through exercise, through repetition, through a blend of learning and reflection that's both painstaking and rewarding. And it takes time.

—Tharp (2006, p. 9)

Practice, optimism, persistence, and positive affirmation are among conditions that contribute to successful habit formation. When we talk about cultivating a *professional practice*, in one sense, the word *practice* implies repetition. To assume that some people are just naturally inclined to succeed, no matter what—that they possess certain innate talents that others do not—is a common misconception—as we know from Dweck (2006), one that can easily turn into an excuse for not practicing, or worse, for quitting altogether. An individual may have natural abilities, strengths, or talents in certain areas, but the most accomplished athletes, musicians, writers, scientists, actors, and CEOs all started somewhere, and they all struggled and failed many times before they got to the top of their respective fields. These individuals forced themselves to do the work, over and over again. They stuck with it. As librarians, we use practice to get better—to develop professionally. We need time to practice, learn, get better, hone our skills, and create the habits that will help us focus on our work and our goals. Good habits reinforce and help motivate practice, and practice is part of what makes habits truly habitual.

When Camila first started her Monday morning journaling, she found herself struggling to make it habitual, but a few things played out in her favor. She was quite optimistic from the beginning, and this feeling increased when she experienced a satisfying jolt of productivity the very first week. She also found that things got easier as she went along. Perseverance paid off. This supports what researchers have found: that one's confidence in the process of developing new habits has a positive effect on success and that sticking with it gets easier as time goes on (Lally, Wardle, & Gardner, 2011, p. 487). Camila has found a time of the week for journaling when she has the break room pretty much to herself. No one is around that early, so she can generally work without interruption. Repetition and familiarity—*routine*, if you will—also help make positive actions habitual.

Something else that helps Camila has to do with the ways she's worked to make this practice a consistent, positive, and focused experience. She does it at the same time and in the same location every week—whenever that's possible—and she always couples the practice with enjoyment of a cup of her favorite tea, providing a reward of sorts. The break room, for Camila, is a "third place" (Oldenburg, 1989), which means that for her it is an ideal place to focus without the usual distractions of home or of her own office. Her Monday morning arrival at work serves as a "cue" for the desired behavior—the thing that serves as a reminder until the routine becomes more automatic (Lally, Wardle, & Gardner, 2011, p. 488). Any event or situation that occurs reliably when the habitual behavior is needed can serve as a cue, or you could use a visual reminder, such as a placard posted in the place where the desired action should take place. When selecting cues for your habit, think about the various different contexts when you would like the desired behavior to occur—and those times when you'd rather avoid it. For instance, when you want to make sorting your email inbox a regular habit, should it be a weekday habit or an *everyday* habit? The answer will determine whether you should select a cue from your office or one that will come up every day, even when you're at home on the weekends. On the other hand, if you'd like to ignore your work email on days off or while you're on vacation, choose a cue that is specific to workdays only. Having worked at this for a year or so now, Camila has come to believe that the most important thing for her is to carry out the practice the same way each week, in the same place—a relatively distraction-free environment, with positive reinforcement—and to build up a regular rhythm and momentum that can carry her through the challenges of the week.

Realistic goal setting and follow-up may also help ensure success. You are aiming for automation, but until you get there, deliberation and self-awareness are needed. Colan and Davis-Colan (2013) suggest focusing on just one new habit at a time, exclusively, at least during the first phase. "The greatest amount of energy and effort is required in the first 21 days as we try to escape the forces that want to pull us back to our old, comfortable ways. But after that, the energy and focus necessary to perform the new habit drops considerably" (p. 179). Researchers Lally and Gardner (2013) suggest regularly monitoring your own behavior and progress as you move forward with the process and garnering support from an encouraging mentor (pp. S151–S152). These proactive and reflective practices can make a big difference as you work on solidifying new behaviors and routine modes of thinking.

Costa and Kallick (2000) lay out a six-step process for adding or changing habits, which incorporates some of the general recommendations we've been discussing: (1) name it; (2) articulate (or draw) descriptions and examples; (3) set realistic, incremental goals; (4) find a way to evaluate progress and incorporate feedback; (5) celebrate success; and (6) persist, even if the change feels awkward (p. 83).

Exercise: Six-Step Habituation

(Adapted from Costa and Kallick [2000, p. 83])

Select one new habit to focus on, and use the following six prompts as a blueprint to help solidify the new practice.

1. Name it:

    • Literally, give it a name.

    • Take this opportunity to share your desire for change with an encouraging mentor or peer.

2. Describe it:

    • What will it look like in practice? Use words or graphics (or better yet, both!).

    • What's the "big why"?—meaning why do you want to cultivate this new habit in the first place?

3. Set realistic goals:

    • These may involve repetition, time, or level of consistency.

    • Try to make these sequential (incremental) rather than simultaneous.

4. Assess and get feedback:

    - How are you feeling about the process?
    - How are you doing relative to your current goal? Does this need adjustment? Is it time to move on to the next goal?
    - Is there anything specific that is getting in the way of your success? Should you make changes to how you practice the new habit (when, where, how, using what cue, etc.)?
    - Is the new behavior, thinking, or response, having the positive impact you imagined? Does the habit itself need adjustment?

5. Celebrate successes:

    - Choose rewards that are significant for you—everyone is different.
    - Consider sharing your celebration with an encouraging mentor or peer.

6. Persist:

    - Remember the "big why."
    - Review and potentially revise the name, descriptive words or graphics, and goals.
    - Repeat steps 4–6 until the new habit is stable and you're ready to take on another.

Steps 1–3 can really give your plan a shape and help make it real. Step 4 rests on the self-awareness and deliberation needed to change ingrained ways of doing things and emphasizes the importance of adaptability. Step 5 is recognition of your drive for success, the challenge of the task, and the positive results of supreme effort. And step 6 reminds us that habit building is a process and that it's important to keep your eye on the goal.

Habits have the potential to help us focus and stay productive even as the pressures of our jobs seem to increase continually and our responsibilities shift and diversify. In part because automatism can dull awareness, it's a good idea to periodically review and revise habitual practices and perhaps identify opportunities for developing new positive routines. Remember that habits can help determine the course of our work and careers, so making sure that those we choose to develop are right for us, in our work context and with our priorities and goals, is very important. Consider which habits will support improved focus, productivity, and thinking, based on the specifics of your own personality and situation. Finally, take care when working to develop and maintain habitual practices—they will serve your purposes best when managed well.

REFERENCES

Allen, D. (2001). *Getting things done: The art of stress-free productivity*. New York, NY: Penguin Books.

Clark, A., & Sousa, B. (2018). *How to be a happy academic: A guide to being effective in research, writing and teaching*. Los Angeles, CA: SAGE.

Colan, L. J., & Davis-Colan, J. (2013). *Stick with it: Mastering the art of adherence*. New York, NY: McGraw-Hill.

Costa, A. L., & Kallick, B. (2000). *Discovering & exploring habits of mind*. Alexandria, VA: Association for Supervision and Curriculum Development.

Covey, S. R. (1990). *The 7 habits of highly effective people: Restoring the character ethic*. New York, NY: Simon and Schuster.

Dweck, C. S. (2006). *Mindset: The new psychology of success*. New York, NY: Random House.

Dweck, C. S. (2014). How can you develop a growth mindset about teaching? *Educational Horizons, 93*(2), 15.

Graybiel, A. M., & Smith, K. S. (2014). Good habits, bad habits. *Scientific American, 310*(6), 38–43.

Kelley, T., & Kelley, D. (2013). *Creative confidence: Unleashing the creative potential within us all*. New York, NY: Crown Business.

Lally, P., & Gardner, B. (2013). Promoting habit formation. *Health Psychology Review, 7*(sup1), S137–S158.

Lally, P., Wardle, J., & Gardner, B. (2011). Experiences of habit formation: A qualitative study. *Psychology, Health & Medicine, 16*(4), 484–489.

Oldenburg, R. (1989). *The great good place: Cafes, coffee shops, community centers, beauty parlors, general stores, bars, hangouts, and how they get you through the day*. New York, NY: Paragon House.

Piper, W., Mateu, F., & Retan, W. (1930). *The easy-to-read little engine that could*. New York, NY: Platt & Munk.

Saunders, E. G. (2018, December 31). The four "attachment styles," and how they sabotage your work-life balance. *New York Times*, p. B5.

Shellenbarger, S. (2003, February 27). Multitasking makes you stupid. *Wall Street Journal*, p. D1.

Silvia, P. (2009). *How to write a lot: A practical guide to productive academic writing*. Washington, DC: American Psychological Association.

Tharp, T. (2006). *The creative habit: Learn it and use it for life*. New York, NY: Simon & Schuster.

5

Telling Our Stories: Using Narrative for Self-Promotion, Professional Development, and Influence

When we tell stories and, just as important, when we listen to the stories of those around us, things just seem to matter more.

—Marek (2011, p. xi)

In order to obtain the funding and buy-in he needs to get customized collections of books into every classroom—those "classroom collections" mentioned in Chapter 1—Marcus has talked to a lot of people. As an educator and historian, he understands the power of dialog and of storytelling. Whenever he, by chance or design, finds himself in the company of a school or district administrator, he tells stories about interesting and exciting projects that underscore the importance of classroom libraries in schools, providing specific context and details he's gleaned from conversations with other library media specialists in his professional network. As he seeks to attract teacher colleagues to his cause, he describes the many ways classroom-based collections can support their curriculum goals across a semester. Finally, as he works with the associate principal to author a grant proposal for a pilot project, he uses narrative to express students' and teachers' needs and the educational and developmental benefits of classroom libraries. He's become somewhat adept at telling stories, employing setting, character, plot, and detail. In the classroom he has found that a narrative can hold an audience of restless teens captive in a certain way, far surpassing the draw of even the most fascinating, and factual, textbook account. There is power in this kind of transmission—the power of engagement and persuasion.

Stories are intricate threads, weaving the past to the present, encompassing our lives and entwining our actions, beliefs, and aspirations, as well as our successes and failures. Stories exist all around us and not just in the texts, movies, and entertainment we consume in our spare time. They are more than fiction and fantasy and fairytale. By telling our stories, we share bits and pieces of ourselves and allow our listeners into our lives on our own terms. Storytelling can be a powerful and effective way to connect with others and build relationships, in the process acquainting the listener with new and diverse environments, situations, roles, and people. In the professional sphere, we use narrative to introduce ourselves, gain recognition for our successes, promote a vision or initiative, or assist us in leading our colleagues or organizations. As a tool for professional development, storytelling helps us talk through and solve problems, develop best practices, and define (or redefine) our own roles and career objectives. Finally, the practice of storytelling can be employed to instruct, spread awareness, or persuade. Mastery of narrative techniques can pay off in so many ways.

The practice of telling stories stretches back in time to before printed alphabets and words, when paintings on the walls of caves depicted the lives and dreams of those living in that era. As language evolved, oral storytelling became a pastime—a form of entertainment and social interaction, an occasion for telling and retelling experience, legend, and myth, for passing these down through generations and across cultures and continents. Some of the most notable tales would eventually be written down and reinterpreted and recorded in multiple languages and formats. There are numerous resources devoted to the history and art of storytelling, but in this chapter, we will present an exploration of storytelling as a professional tool, looking at narrative structure and some of the key elements that go into making a story, telling autobiographical stories, using storytelling to inform and persuade, and telling stories to support getting the work done. Librarians' personal and collective stories, when used in strategic ways and in opportune situations, can enhance both effectiveness and career satisfaction.

STRUCTURE AND ELEMENTS

You've been studying the art of storytelling ever since your parents read you bedtime stories. You already know what the structure of a good story is. All you need is to be reminded. The simplest way to remember is to start with these words, "Once upon a time, there was . . ."

—Smith (2012, p. 55)

Do you remember sitting by a campfire as a kid and telling ghost stories? Or playing the "pass the story" game, where one person started with a character, or event, or setting and passed the narrative off to the next person who would add more details—and so on around the circle—until someone threw in a conclusion? Telling stories and collaborating on stories can be fun, but what makes a story good? What types of narrative will accomplish our objectives in a professional context? A professional story is not a novel or a poem, but that doesn't mean it has to be bland or boring. How do the most adept storytellers engage their audiences? What are some of the structures and elements we should think about when developing our own stories? Strategic use of plot, tension, surprise, transformation, and universal themes or ideas can keep the narrative alive and make for more engaging professional stories.

The *Oxford English Dictionary* (*OED*) defines *narrative* as "an account of a series of events, facts, etc., given in order and with the establishing of connections between them; a narration, a story, an account" (Narrative, 2003). Narrative is basically the "establishing of connections"—when we tell a story, we connect the pieces together. The starting point of a narrative plot is usually a description of a situation—the calm before the storm, if you will—and from there a storyteller introduces settings, characters, events, tension in the form of challenges or obstacles, and in the end—almost always—some form of resolution. Aristotle, the fourth century BC philosopher, believed that, in a tragedy, events should relate to one another in a certain way, with a three-part structure: *beginning, middle,* and *end* (*Poetics*, Section VII). We all recognize this three-part structure as we reflect on stories we've told and heard. Joy, for instance, mentors students at her former library school and often tells the story of her own transition from web designer to public librarian. She begins by talking about life in the tech services firm—the day-to-day challenges, the things she liked and didn't like about going to work, and what it felt like to find herself unexpectedly on the job market. This is the setup, the initial status quo. She ends by describing the professional satisfaction she garners in her current public library position. The connecting narrative—what happened on the way from point A to point B—provides a case study about the challenges of finding direction and finding a career and about strategies employed along the way, information that could be very useful for those coming out of library school or anyone who finds themselves in the job market. One of the things this beginning-middle-end model suggests is that there is a return to stasis or a new status quo—a degree of calm or stability in both

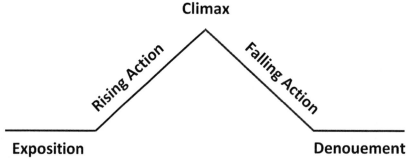

Figure 5.1 Diagram of Freytag's Pyramid

the beginning and the end, with tension, action, challenge, and transformation in the middle of the story. We use this beginning-middle-end structure, or variations of it, all the time. Becoming more aware of the plot structures we use, and employing them deliberately and strategically, can help clarify our stories and ultimately make them more impactful for our audiences.

Gustav Freytag, a German writer in the late 1800s, developed a five-part elaboration of beginning-middle-end (Figure 5.1): (1) *exposition*—providing details about character and initial situation; (2) *rising action*—as tension builds; (3) *climax*; (4) *falling action*—as loose ends are tied up and tension wanes; and (5) *denouement*—when the resolution is made clear (MacEwan, 1900, pp. 114–115).

Freytag's rising action implies mounting complications and the tension that goes along with it. It is suspenseful; no resolution in sight. The climax of the story is a turning point, the beginning of the end. During falling action, tension decreases as certain complications are worked out, and during the *denouement* (a resolution, or conclusion), a new status quo is defined. Building a rising action, climax, and falling action structure into the middle of a story provides suspense and an ah-ha! moment for the listener or reader. This effect can be incorporated into professional narratives, just as it can as the basis for a compelling murder mystery.

EXERCISE: FIVE-PART NARRATIVE

1. Think of an initiative that has been or would be beneficial in a specific way for library patrons. You could use an initiative that you have been involved with in the past or one you believe would benefit your patrons/

clients in the present. If you do not have past experience or a current position in a library, think about a hypothetical situation based on what you have learned about the challenges patrons/clients face in a specific library setting.

2. In a journal, respond to the following prompts (substitute the future tense in place of past tense as appropriate for your perspective):

Exposition	What was the status quo before the initiative? How were library staff and patrons affected by the situation?
Rising action	What solution did you envision? What were the challenges to implementation? What happened leading up to the deciding moment? Linger a bit on the uncertainties to bring these to life, and help build a little suspense.
Climax	Describe the moment when a new realization was made, or when a major challenge was overcome, or even when things changed decisively for the worse. How did you come to the realization? What was your "everything became clear" moment?
Falling action	Once the climax passed, what happened? How did the loose ends begin coming together?
Denouement	Describe the new status quo. What ultimate impact did the events of the narrative have? How have staff and patrons been affected by the change?

3. Consider whether the story you're telling has a single arc of beginning-middle-end, with a single climax, or if it might be better suited to a series of narrative arcs with a few twists and turns. You can adjust accordingly by conceiving your story as a sequence of episodes, each with its own arc.

4. Review your narrative, and read it out loud. Realize that you may need to make adjustments for tone. Although any story can benefit from a little suspense, launching a new classroom collection program is *not actually* a murder mystery.

Freytag's five-part narrative arc is just one variation on the beginning-middle-end structure. Another way to think about it is through Olson's (2015) ABT or And-But-Therefore structure, which uses the relationships between different story elements (*and/but*) to bring the reader to a particular conclusion (*therefore*). In the book, *Houston, We Have a Narrative: Why Science Needs a Story*, Olson proposes building stories by weaving together a few facts, joined by *and* (exposition), and then throwing a wrench into the works with *but*. "*But* is a contradiction word that causes the narrative flow to switch direction," thereby establishing a problem and ushering us into the middle of the narrative structure (pp. 97–98). Subsequently, a *therefore* introduces a conclusion or a new status quo. There is a simplicity to this paradigm, which can support setting, plot, characters, and complexity, whether as an extensive narrative or as a one-sentence "elevator speech" (more about elevator speeches later).

Exercise: One-Sentence ABT

(Adapted from Olson [2015, pp. 95–99])

Use Marcus's example ABT narrative to build your own. Think of a story you'd like to tell about a work situation. Begin by laying out the facts and details using *and*. Introduce an inciting action with *but*, and use *therefore* to spell out the resolution.

Example—from Marcus

Miss Jackson and I were talking the other day about the importance of nurturing students' curiosities. . .

and

. . . she'd like to be able to refer to, pull from, and suggest a variety of STEM-related books during off-the-cuff classroom discussion, when students are most engaged, *and* she'd like students to be able to browse various related books to select their own supplemental readings. . .

but

. . . logistics dictate that access to these types of materials via the school library is much too limited and controlled to support such curiosity-driven, in-the-moment use. . .

therefore

. . . I'd like to propose that she and I build a pilot classroom collection next semester and then assess for learning and developmental outcomes.

For Olson, the ABT structure is "the DNA of story" (p. 96), with origins in Aristotle and the genesis of beginning-middle-end. The one-sentence narrative you developed through this exercise could stand alone as a story, in and of itself, or might serve as the basis for a more complex and layered telling.

In addition to the beginning-middle-end *structural* form, Choy (2017) outlines three additional categories of story components: (1) *elemental components*—things that are somewhat universal in the art of storytelling, like archetypal characters, challenges, or journeys; (2) *authentic components*—where "a story reveals a genuine part of the teller, which, in turn, elicits emotion in the audience"; and (3) *strategic components*—strategic in that the story engages the imagination and thereby motivates action (p. 6). A "hook," reflection, and an ending that serves the purpose of the story are among the key elements for Choy (pp. 13–17), who goes on to outline three great ways to "hook" your audience, called the "3Cs": conflict (some sort of opposing needs—whether of epic proportions or more pedestrian); contrast (juxtaposition of opposites); or contradiction (something that confounds the audience's expectations). This hook is often unsettling or surprising for the listener, capturing their attention and engaging them right at the start of the story. Choy also suggests that making your own reflective practice visible in the story can help drive home your narrative's theme and recommends making a deliberate choice regarding whether the conclusion is left open to interpretation (when you want to invite the audience to share their own perspectives) or closed (when you want to leave no doubt in the audience's mind about the practical implications of the story).

Hook, reflection, and choice of ending can play out in a million different ways in combination. For example, in Joy's "back on my feet" story about her transition from one career to another, she hooks her mentees right at the beginning by contrasting life as a successful digital designer with what it was like to find herself unexpectedly out on her own and scrambling to figure out what would come next in her career. In relating the sequence of events that led her to choose public librarianship, Joy alternates between talking about events as they happened to her and describing her own reflective thinking process. For instance, she alternates narrative about her discussions with different professionals to figure out what kind of work she ultimately wanted to do with some descriptions of how she reflectively weighed the pros and cons of different possible career tracks. This lets her audience in on her thought process and reinforces one of the themes of her story—that the people with whom we network can play important roles in career decision-making. It helps her listeners realize that the decisions she made were things she really thought about carefully, and it gets them invested in her way of thinking. Finally, Joy usually ends this particular story by drawing some connections between her own journey and the specific situation her mentee may be experiencing, hoping to spark a conversation about the mentee's own interpretation of the outcome; in other words, she gives her narrative an "open" ending.

Exercise: Core Components

(Adapted from Choy [2017])

1. Look back at either your five-elements story or your ABT story.

2. **Hook:** Refine the opening of your story or develop a new one using one of the "3C" "hook" options:

   - *Conflict*—Are there characters or groups who have opposing needs right at the beginning of your story, something that can set up a grand challenge for your protagonist?

   - *Contrast*—Is there some striking difference between two individuals or elements of the story? This could be a before/after comparison, for example.

   - *Contradiction*—Is there something about the situation of your story that will seem counterintuitive or surprising to your audience?

3. **Reflection:** Review the sequence of events and narrative arc of your story to identify the moments that required reflective thinking on the part of the protagonist. Think about ways to draw your listener into the thought process during these episodes—for instance, "I couldn't believe . . ." or "I wasn't sure . . ." or "This meant that . . ." Although you may identify many such moments, you will ultimately want to use these passages selectively, just enough to engage the empathy of your listener.

4. **Strategic ending:** Consider the purpose of your story—what lessons or takeaways do you hope your listeners will end up with? Or is this a story that merely draws the listener toward a resolution but ultimately relies on *their* interpretation to determine the ending? Based on your answers to these questions, refine or revise your narrative to include either a "closed" or an "open" ending.

5. Read your revised narrative out loud. Multiple revisions may be required to accomplish these purposes with some subtlety. These techniques should be engaging and should match your purpose, but if overdone, they can sometimes come off as somewhat manipulative.

You might want to make consideration of these three elements—hook, reflection, and strategic ending—an explicit part of your process when planning to use storytelling in professional situations. After you've used these techniques, reflect on how they may have impacted your audience. With practice, you will become more adept at employing them routinely and effectively.

There are a few more features that could help ensure the success of your stories. The first is depiction of some type of *transformation*—whether for the individual, the group or organization, the patron, or the world. Stories that truly engage often provide a greater understanding of something, and the good stories—the ones we most remember—will portray transformation. "Audiences innately want to know not just what happened in the story, but what's different at the end, and why" (Choy, 2017, p. 15). In the beginning of her metamorphosis story, Joy was not only more or less satisfied but also quite ambivalent about her work as a digital designer, and she went through a series of key experiences as the story played out. But what her mentees really want to know is: How have her life and outlook changed? What has made the difference? The practical lessons from this narrative derive from the challenges and strategies of the journey, but much of the satisfaction comes from the realization of transformation.

In addition, employing situations, issues, or themes that are somewhat *universal* can help people connect with your story. You want to find ways to help your listeners relate cognitively and/or emotionally with the people or situations of your tale. Simmons (2006) emphasizes that good stories, whether factual or not, always have an element of Truth, with a capital *T*, the kind of truth that somehow manages to align with what we generally already believe to be true about the world. For example, "Puppies make us feel good. Love hurts. Resentment keeps the wrong person awake at night" (p. 32). Weaving into your story something that connects with the beliefs and aspirations of your audience ". . . acts like a tuning fork. Your listeners resonate with that Truth, remember their own experiences, and tune in to you and your message" (p. 32). For instance, if you asked the teachers and administrators who listen to Marcus's stories what they consider to be of greatest importance in secondary education, chances are that most of them would point to student learning and development—a concern developed during years, or even decades, of teaching. This is why Marcus's narratives so often include emblematic descriptions of classroom challenges and emphasize transformative learning. If we want our audience to believe us, to connect with us, to follow along with our narratives, we should help them somehow recognize versions of themselves in our stories, their past experiences, their beliefs, and their concerns.

Finally, keeping in mind who your *audience* is, along with what your objective is vis-à-vis that audience, will ensure that your story is not just good but also that it accomplishes what you hope it will. Storytellers who are focused on their own motivations could easily forget about their audience and how those individuals might be responding to the story they are hearing (Choy, 2017, p. 9). Before we start to speak or write, we need to think about who will be listening to us or reading our narrative and why—not just why we *want* them to listen but also why they *would*. This knowledge can influence tone, specificity, length of story, and format (off-the-cuff remark, essay, article, chapter, book, etc.). Marcus's stories about the purposes and possibilities of his proposed initiative vary greatly according to who his target audience is: supervisors, district officials, classroom teachers, grant organizations, and so forth.

EXERCISE: "LET ME TELL YOU A STORY . . ."

1.   Think of a work-related story that informs or illustrates something about you or some aspect of your job/role.

2.   In a journal, write the story, starting with the phrase "Let me tell you a story about . . ." Utilize a narrative structure with beginning (exposition), middle (tension), and end (resolution).

3.   Revise the story for different audiences, such as the following:

   •   Your supervisor/boss
   •   The people you supervise
   •   Your coworker/colleague
   •   People who are interviewing you for a new position

4.   Consider: How is each story different? Why? What did you leave out or add for each person/group? How do you think these different audiences will react to your story?

There are many different situations that call for pitching the same story differently for different professional audiences. This exercise could prove particularly useful whenever you are trying to garner support across your organization for a particular initiative or setting the groundwork for a big career move.

STORYTELLING FOR SELF-KNOWLEDGE AND SELF-PROMOTION

As creatures of time, who both want and need to communicate our lives in time, it seems we can do no other than tell a story.

—Randall (1995, p. 87)

Perhaps the most important story you need to develop and be able to tell is your own story—something that both defines you and helps others understand you. This means not only your professional biography—who you are and how you "came to be," in a professional sense—but also the stories about how you work—the ways you handle responsibilities and challenges. Through stories we contextualize, personalize, and characterize our daily lives and work, our experiences, and our goals, thus making sense of the world around us and of our place in it. As journalist and author Joan Didion famously wrote, "We tell ourselves stories in order to live" (1979, p. 11).

We glance backward and then forward, with a stronger understanding of where we come from and a better idea of our potential future selves.

In the professional arena, you will want to tell your own story as it defines your work, your skills, your experience, and your goals, what Hansen (2009) refers to as the quintessential "you story," a tool for both self-promotion and self-knowledge (p. 9). You will be able to "sell yourself" better in certain circumstances, but first and foremost, you will gain a deeper understanding of your own professional narrative, your journey thus far, and your future pathways. Remember that you can—and do—have more than one story to tell. Professionals need to talk and write about themselves in different ways and in many different situations. Perhaps the most common "you story" is the professional biography.

EXERCISE: PROFESSIONAL BIOGRAPHY OUTLINE

This outline can serve as a resource for preparing to talk or write about yourself, your work, and your aspirations in many different contexts.

1. In a journal brainstorm ideas and information related to your professional life. Use the following prompts to get started:

   - Describe what inspired you to work in libraries or become a librarian/information professional.
   - Who has influenced you the most in your career, and how?
   - Describe the aspects of your job/career that are the most satisfying.
   - What are some of the most formative experiences you've had professionally?
   - What are you still curious about—what do you still want to learn, and why?

2. Develop a bulleted outline incorporating the things from this list that you deem most significant.

   - Put some thought into the selection and sequencing of material.
   - Remember that this outline is a "catchall" collection—editing and resequencing will happen later in the process, when you're developing different versions of your story.
   - Consider including timelines, stories within stories, and different perspectives.

Once you have a professional biography outline, you can draw on that to create individual, spin-off "you stories" that illustrate and highlight specific skills, experiences, and accomplishments. You will be able to develop multiple narratives demonstrating different aspects of your character, to be used in different circumstances, for different audiences (Hansen, 2009, p. 9).

Discussing the one-sentence ABT story structure earlier, we mentioned the notion of the *elevator speech*. This is a brief verbal summary (archetypically the length of an elevator ride). Your "you story" elevator speech describes who you are and what you do, for the purpose of introducing yourself to people you may want to impress, such as supervisors, new network connections, future colleagues, or potential employers. It is basically a pared-down version of your "you story," designed to take advantage of a very small window of opportunity. These pitches may touch on strengths, goals, ambitions, and your current work situation. Elevator speeches are great when you have just a few moments to "sell yourself." However, because of the brevity, designing a narrative structure or arc can be tricky.

Exercise: "You Story" Elevator Speech

1. Go back and review the professional biography outline from the earlier exercise. Based on individual(s) you are likely to speak with in a specific situation (your supervisor, a fellow conference attendee, a potential employer), write down the five most compelling points of interest from the outline, in no particular order.

1.
2.
3.
4.
5.

2. Now think about sequence and transitions: Perhaps there is a small narrative arc; if not, what arrangement would make your point most clear? Most persuasive?

3. Read your draft out loud and time it. Trim it if it's over two minutes, and if it's under two minutes, consider adding just the teeniest bit of texture, detail, or narrative arc.

4. Practice reading your elevator pitch out loud. Work toward using an appropriate conversational tone.

5. Try practicing your delivery with a supportive peer or mentor.

The elevator speech format will also be useful for you when you are try-ing to market library services or garner support for a particular initiative, as Marcus has been doing to drum up support for his project. And they can be used as advocacy tools, to explain how you and your library provide value to the community and to your specific clientele. You can simply reuse the previous exercise, substituting compelling information related to the topic, or audience, or questions, at hand. Amir, who often gets asked what he does in his special librarian job, has a prepared answer—elevator speech-style—ready as a response: "I help the finance professionals in my organization stay informed and current on relevant financial news and the business activities of competitive firms so they are better prepared to do their jobs, and I curate and maintain a knowledgebase of data and records to document the history of, ensure the health of, and promote the growth of the organization." As a professional, it's a great idea to have a number of elevator speeches at the ready—you never know when you could unexpect-edly have the ear of a stakeholder or new contact.

In addition to telling stories about who you are, from time to time you will find yourself in situations where you're asked to speak with supervi-sors, potential employers, or promotion and tenure committees about the details of how you have handled specific situations or challenges, over-come obstacles, solved problems, mastered certain skills or tools, or worked with others to achieve a specific goal/outcome/result. When she first interviewed to be a reference librarian, Joy was asked to describe an experience in which she had interacted with a frustrated member of the public and to discuss strategies she employed to resolve the situation. Drawing on her experience interacting with clients at the digital design firm, she talked about a specific encounter she had when she was trouble-shooting a navigational problem for a client. The interview question Joy was responding to—"Was there a time . . . and how did you handle. . .?"—is what's referred to as a situational or behavioral question (versus one based on knowledge or opinion). Other examples include the following:

- Tell us about a time when you've been given primary responsibility for organizing and managing a specific initiative.
- Give an example of a time when you were under some stress and really needed to rely on your own coping skills to be successful.
- Describe a project you worked on that failed. What would you do dif-ferently, or what did you learn?
- What is your thinking on [some important current issue in the field]? How would you approach a related initiative?

You can probably tell from these questions or prompts that they are practi-cally begging for narrative. There are a few structural models out there that can assist you in developing narrative responses to behavioral questions, including the STAR model (Situation, Task, Action, Result). Note that if you are asked a behavioral question and there is an area of experience you want to cover that has *not* been a part of your personal professional past—in other words, if you are a student, a novice librarian, or even a veteran contemplating a new area of work—it is fine in most cases to discuss hypothetical situations, as long as you make clear to your listeners that, although you haven't had this experience yet, this is something you've been thinking about—you've thought about it because you understand how important it is, and because of that thinking, you have some real solutions in mind. And the important thing is to make these stories as concrete as possible based on your informed understanding of that hypothetical.

Exercise: STAR Worksheet

Use Joy's example STAR narrative to build your own.

1. Think about a specific behavioral situation you may be asked (or want) to talk about.

2. Develop a list of keywords or concepts related to each of the STAR prompts, as given next.

3. Add in narrative to make it into a story. Include details such as setting (where and when), characters (who), and a timeline that illustrates the action (what you did) and result (conclusion and aftermath).

Example Narrative—from Joy

	Keywords	Narrative
Situation	• Longtime client • Usability problems • Technical problems • Tried client services representative (CSR)—still frustrated • Supervisor turned to Joy	I ended up speaking on the phone with a client who had become extremely frustrated trying to give us feedback on a newly designed interface. This client was understandably frustrated because they were having a problem with a site we were creating for them; they were thinking about how their customers might feel! To top it all off, there had apparently been an exchange with one of our client services representatives (or CSRs) that ended in misunderstanding and even more frustration, so my supervisor put me on the line.

	Keywords	Narrative
Task	• Determine exact nature of the problem(s) • Solve the issues that were frustrating the client • Reassure the client—re: customer service as well as product	I knew I had to (1) figure out what the issue was with the design or the technology, (2) fix it, and (3) reassure the client about the design *and* about the ability of our customer service department to respond quickly to any future issues.
Action	• Reassurance first! • Screen-sharing tool to see client's interface/demo solutions • Helped correct a browser issue • Refined the interface design • Trained CSR for future	So, the first thing I did was start with reassurance, letting the client know that we would absolutely be able to fix the problem! Then I used a screen-sharing tool, so I could actually see the problem they were experiencing on their computer and also show potential solutions. I noticed an issue with the browser and helped to update that. We ultimately decided to adjust a few things in the interface design for usability. And, finally, I spent a few minutes talking to the CSR, clarifying what the issue was to help with future communication.
Result	• Happy client • Happy supervisor • Better prepared CSR	I think responding with confidence and reassurance was key for helping to de-escalate the frustration of the client. This was a good resolution for everyone—it saved the client relationship. I think it really made my supervisor happy, and (most important) in the end, the CSR had the training and the confidence to handle this type of issue in the future.

4. Read your STAR narrative out loud, and make sure you can deliver it in an appropriate conversational tone.
5. Try practicing your delivery with a supportive peer or mentor.

You'll find that behavioral questions will come up in so many situations—from job interviews to day-to-day problem solving to proposals for projects or promotions. Try thinking about potential behavioral questions and developing brief lists of STAR keywords in preparation. Also, if you can internalize the STAR method, you'll be able to fall back on it—so that it comes to mind whenever an unexpected behavioral question or prompt comes your way.

You probably realize by now that you need to be able to introduce yourself—along with your skills, experiences, and accomplishments—not only in person (e.g., in an interview) but in writing as well (e.g., in a cover or promotion letter). Your "you story" and behavioral narratives should infuse your résumé, cover letter, tenure and promotion file, and even your online professional profiles. When you approach writing in these situations, consider where it might be advantageous to include narrative-arc descriptions—about how you chose librarianship, the formative experiences that shaped how you respond to challenges or relate to others, your aspirations for the future, and so forth. For job hunters, the cover letter may be the best opportunity to introduce yourself, narratively, to a potential employer. These documents provide context for your experience and skills, allowing for explanation, details, and anecdotes. They complement the résumé or CV and can demonstrate personality, depth, and creativity. The personal narratives required for many tenure and promotion portfolios, or for formal performance evaluation processes, function similarly. Use narrative to personalize your work history and tell a story that demonstrates your interests and experience. Consider using narrative to illustrate how you have used a specific resource, how you spearheaded a certain initiative, how you overcame a specific challenge, or how you landed your current role.

STORYTELLING TO GET THE WORK DONE

The average person today is inundated with facts and data, and we let most of this pass through our brains with minimal retention or reaction— unless something makes the information stand out in a meaningful way. That's where story comes in.

—Choy (2017, p. xvi)

So far we've covered how to use storytelling strategically to accomplish personal objectives—to persuade, establish, and build a professional reputation or obtain a position or career advancement. But good narrative technique can also be applied to support the work we do day-to-day. Here we are referring mostly to expository storytelling, when narrative is used to explain or describe—it's another way to think about workplace communication. As librarians, the heart and soul of what we do is helping others find and utilize information and resources. We provide reference and instruction assistance, we develop programs and systems, and we organize and arrange our resources and our spaces to be conducive to our patrons' needs and preferences. To accomplish all of this, no matter what kind of library we work in, we need to communicate effectively, collaborate, and interact productively with patrons, clients, colleagues, supervisors, staff, and vendors. Effective internal and external communication is critical. Narrative technique can be employed in these situations, be they formal meetings or informal gatherings. We can use stories in our workshops, classes, or training sessions; we can even use them at the reference desk. The stories we tell one another in the workplace can also increase understanding and contribute to a more open and healthy workplace (Saltmarshe, 2018, p. 6). By employing explanatory or descriptive narrative in key situations, we help break down differences, promote empathy and cohesion, and enhance and build knowledge collectively. We'll look first at strategies for weaving a highly engaging expository narrative and then consider a few specific practices: organizational storytelling, narratives specifically addressing a public audience, and the gathering of library users' own stories.

Expository narrative must accurately describe and inform but will do so most effectively when it is truly engaging. *TED Talks*, a format cultivated and popularized since the mid-1980s by producers at TED, is a term that has come to signify brevity and engagement in presentation style. Anderson, in *TED Talks: The Official TED Guide to Public Speaking* (2016), provides five principles for using narrative to explain complex issues in a limited period of time. To begin with, (1) start "right where you are"—in the here and now, with your initial exposition. Then, (2) spark "a fire called *curiosity*"—throw in something that forces your audience to ask themselves questions, like *why?* and *how?* So as not to overwhelm, (3) bring "in concepts one by one"—gradually illuminating key pieces of the puzzle as you build up toward a major concept or a big reveal. Also, (4) think specifically about using metaphor and analogy to help your audience draw connections between the reality you are building narratively and their own mental model(s) of the world. Finally, (5) use examples to illustrate your ideas (pp. 76–77).

Exercise: Drawing Them In

(Adapted from Anderson [2016, pp. 76–77])

1. In a journal jot down the basic facts related to a project you're currently involved in or one that you would be interested in proposing.

2. Brainstorm possible story elements based on the following prompts:

"Start where you are."	What is the situation right now? Are there issues your library users or staff are experiencing that could be addressed productively by this project? What are their experiences?
"Light a fire called curiosity."	Can you point to a gap in knowledge or understanding? Something unsettling? It may be helpful to think back to Choy's (2017) "3Cs"—conflict, contrast, or contradiction.
"Bring in concepts one at a time."	If you can identify the main point, or "big reveal," or climax of your story, what concepts will the audience need to encounter and understand along the way? Draw them along.
"Use metaphors and analogies."	Think about the people and situations in your story, and identify connections to your audience's experiences and beliefs.
"Use examples."	Identify possible little stories (stories within stories) related to your narrative.

3. In your journal, sketch out a draft, drawing on the ideas you've brainstormed.
4. Try practicing your delivery with a supportive peer or mentor.

Storytelling techniques such as these can and should be used in everyday professional contexts. They will help you convey practical information and will also allow you to express a little bit of what you feel or believe about the topic at hand.

Storytelling is used organizationally to communicate, make sense of, and collaboratively develop mission, vision, and strategy. When we think about "organizational storytelling," a few different things come to mind. First, if you scratch the surface, every organization—every library—has a founding story or myth, complete with characters, conflict, and narrative arc, with adversity, survival, and transformation at its heart. Then there are the ways the organization defines its mission, goals, and the scope of its activities. These organizational stories are shared internally and may also be used to depict the organization publicly. They are deployed at all levels but are often seen as directed primarily by the institution's leadership team. Forman (2013) points out the appeal of narrative for organizational leaders, not only because of its power to influence but also because of its capacity to help individuals make sense of things (p. 5). However,

Forman also emphasizes the need to incorporate all stakeholders' voices into these narratives, including the voices of employees and clients (patrons). "This requires the storyteller, whether an individual or an organization, to begin the activity by listening" (p. 26). Organizational storytelling is a shared responsibility. Individuals who do the work of the organization, and those who benefit from its services—in this case the library's patrons and community—will likely have some impact on the story the organization tells about itself, even if that contribution is difficult to define.

In the workplace, we need to tell each other our own stories, of course, and share our perspectives on the organization's narratives, but we also need to listen to others tell their stories so that we can learn from one another, strengthen bonds, share knowledge, and cultivate understanding and empathy within our working relationships. Effective two-way communication builds confidence and creates a safe and supportive environment for problem solving, exploration, collaboration, and creativity. Because we are so often pulled in multiple directions, and have many things on our minds, it can be difficult to fully give our attention to one another. Choy (2017) talks about the benefits of "listening aggressively" as others speak (pp. 140–147):

- Think like a film director. Use your imagination to visualize the speaker's story.

- Listen with your whole body (except your mouth!). Be aware of your limbs, your movements, and your gaze.

- Feel what they feel. Use body language to signify empathy, without exaggeration.

- Paraphrase and ask clarifying questions. If you want more evidence or clarification, speak up.

- Don't interject with your own story. Keep focus on the storyteller by resisting the urge to immediately verbalize the connections you're drawing between their story and your own experience.

- Be both curious and respectful. You may find that this helps others feel more comfortable and more willing to share openly.

You can also ask questions and share anecdotes to help encourage reticent coworkers, staff, and supervisors. The next time you have a discussion with a colleague, ask them to provide more details and expand on a thought or description. Intentional two-way communication is a habit that can be cultivated and should eventually become second nature. Formalizing opportunities to share narratives can help establish a culture of storytelling within the organization.

EXERCISE: STORYTELLING GROUP

A storytelling group can be comprised of a variety of people in your own workplace or colleagues from other libraries or organizations. It can be an organized group that meets regularly or an impromptu session of whoever is around at the time. In other words, don't overthink it, and have fun.

1. Set up a storytelling group with colleagues, asking each person to tell a work-related story (give a time limit of five minutes, max). Use prompts that can assist, such as the following: When was the last time you felt like you accomplished something significant? Tell us about an "aha!" moment? How did you get the job you have now? Who is your favorite person to work with, and why?

2. Listeners should have time to respond, comment, ask questions, and discuss.

3. Collaborate to find ways to use these stories as jumping off points for research, writing, new initiatives, professional development, or outreach.

There also may be various occasions for sharing stories about your professional practice with those outside of your organization—with colleagues who play some role in our profession, yes, but also with individuals who are not librarians and do not work in or around libraries. By telling others about our work—for instance, new initiatives, recent donations, technological advancements, or daily workflow and procedures—we can develop narratives that have the power to defy stereotypes, invite discussion, and transform the status quo. At the same time, we can cultivate understanding and promote our libraries, institutions, and profession.

When we share our professional insight publicly, we become, in a sense, public scholars—individuals who connect with members of the community in matters related to intellectual, professional, and institutional practice. There are many outlets for external communication and storytelling, such as open discussion groups, town hall meetings, workshops, and meetup groups. One idea you might try is sharing through informed opinion pieces submitted for publication in newspapers, trade magazines, newsletters, and blogs.

EXERCISE: WRITE AN OPINION PIECE

(Adapted from Jensen [2017, pp. 155–156])

Write an essay/article about something related to your workplace (e.g., a project or initiative you are working on), a library where you may be a patron, or libraries in general. Use the following "op-ed" structure, as defined by Jensen:

1. Open with an anecdote (a short, amusing, or interesting story about a real incident, issue, or person).
2. Make your overall argument.
3. Back it up with evidence.
4. Add a "to be sure" paragraph that acknowledges counterarguments.
5. Build your conclusion (circling back to comment on the original anecdote or argument).

Writing opinion pieces is an effective way to break into public scholarship. We can adapt our language, style, and tone to spread awareness of a specific idea or concept, garner support for a specific project or initiative, and influence and persuade our audience(s) in ways that will benefit our work and our libraries. It is important to present our evidence as engaging stories and to be able to communicate our scholarship and writing to a wider audience in ways that make sense to them (Jensen, 2017, p. 156).

Our patrons' stories can also have a significant influence on our library's services, resources, and collections. Patron needs and expectations are always changing and may be quite diverse depending on the type of library, community, and situation. Users' stories, both personal and collective, can inform and influence our decisions and strategic initiatives. Informal ways to gather their stories can be as simple as asking colleagues about their experiences with patrons or approaching patrons and asking specific questions: How did you enjoy this event? What did you learn from this class? How do you feel about this resource/service/space? What collections do you use the most? More formal methods may involve organizing a focus group, or a storytelling event, like the one described previously for colleagues. Or you could erect a story booth in your library where patrons can record themselves. You might want to pass out story-gathering forms for patrons to fill out or put up online surveys with targeted questions and feedback options (Margolis & Drury, n.d.).

Working in libraries, we are surrounded by stories on the shelves, stories of our patrons and clients, stories of our colleagues, stories of our stakeholders and our leaders, and our own stories—narratives that can help us understand who we are, what we want, and where we are going. Through narrative we create stronger networks while bridging divides and flattening silos. We enhance reality and help contextualize and humanize information and data. We are able to better understand and share our organization's structure and vision. By taking control of our own storyline, and strategically sharing bits and pieces of it in a variety of situations and for a variety of audiences, we can better control our present and steer our work and careers toward the future we envision.

REFERENCES

Anderson, C. (2016). *TED Talks: The official TED guide to public speaking*. Boston, MA: Houghton Mifflin Harcourt.

Choy, E. (2017). *Let the story do the work: The art of storytelling for business*. New York, NY: American Management Association.

Didion, J. (1979). *The white album*. New York, NY: Simon and Schuster.

Forman, J. (2013). *Storytelling in business: The authentic and fluent organization*. Stanford, CA: Stanford Business Books.

Hansen, K. (2009). *Tell me about yourself: Storytelling to get jobs and propel your career*. Indianapolis, IN: JIST Publishing.

Jensen, J. (2017). *Write no matter what: Advice for academics*. Chicago, IL: The University of Chicago Press.

MacEwan, E. J. (1900) [Copyright 1894]. *Freytag's technique of the drama, an exposition of dramatic composition and art by Dr. Gustav Freytag: An authorized translation from the sixth German edition* (3rd ed.). Chicago, IL: Scott, Foresman and Company.

Marek, K. (2011). *Organizational storytelling for librarians: Using stories for effective leadership*. Chicago, IL: ALA Editions.

Margolis, M., & Drury, K. (n.d.). The library story: A strategic storytelling toolkit for public libraries. Retrieved from https://www.powerlibrary.org/librarians/special-projects-office-of-commonwealth-libraries/the-library-story-a-strategic-storytelling-toolkit-for-public-libraries/

Narrative. (2003). In *Oxford English dictionary (3rd ed.)*. Retrieved from http://www.oed.com/view/Entry/125146?result=1&rskey=ntFuBY&

Olson, R. (2015). *Houston, we have a narrative: Why science needs a story*. Chicago, IL: The University of Chicago Press.

Randall, W. L. (1995). *The stories we are: An essay on self-creation*. Toronto, Canada: University of Toronto Press.

Saltmarshe, E. (2018). Using story to change systems. *Stanford Social Innovation Review*. Retrieved from https://ssir.org/articles/entry/using_story_to_change_systems

Simmons, A. (2006). *The story factor: Secrets of influence from the art of storytelling*. Cambridge, MA: Basic Books.

Smith, P. (2012). *Lead with a story: A guide to crafting business narratives that captivate, convince, and inspire*. New York, NY: American Management Association.

6

Finding Your Place: Mindfulness and Self-Compassion

If you do not feel yourself growing in your work and your life broadening and deepening, if your task is not a perpetual tonic to you, you have not found your place.

—Marden (1907, p. 45)

Sana was offered the chance to take on some new responsibilities in the academic library where she works, when one of her colleagues retired during a college-wide hiring freeze. Although it was a new area of work for her, she was the logical candidate to take on management of electronic resources, due to her technical skills and knowledge of library systems. And Sana loves a new challenge. Her constant desire for variety and learning new skills keeps her energized, and she knew that this would be an exciting venture, as well as something to add to her résumé. At first, she dove into manuals and articles and researched competencies, best practices, and the nature and lifecycle of electronic resources. She joined email lists, connected with e-resources librarians at other institutions, and spent hours trying to learn about the systems and tools that she would be working with. It wasn't long before she started to worry that she might never be able to learn all that she needed to know in order to do the job. She began to do the work—quite well, by any objective measure. But she felt like an imposter in her new role. Increasingly, she was being pressured by colleagues to do more, fix this, troubleshoot that, and do it all ASAP. Moreover, she was still involved in acquisitions and cataloging and didn't want to give up her reference desk shift. She lacked a positive support structure and had not received adequate training for her new role. She found herself actively avoiding colleagues and her library director for fear that they might press her on project updates and status reports or ask her to do more than she was capable of doing. She was overwhelmed and frustrated and felt like she'd lost her way.

What Sana was feeling is not unique. No work environment is perfect, and that dream job may never come to fruition—at least not in the way you imagine it. So what do you do when the frustration creeps in and the position that was supposed to bring energy and fulfillment brings misgivings instead? How do we slow down, assess our state of well-being, and become more aware of what's going on around us? More aware of how we are responding? How can we cultivate more positivity and better self-esteem? And how can we find energy and satisfaction in our current roles while minimizing stress? In this chapter, we will explore these questions and offer ways to enhance confidence, mindfulness, and self-compassion in our professional lives.

CONFIDENCE

For the record, you don't have to feel especially "successful" to relate to the dichotomy of the public face of confidence and competence on the one hand and the private voices of self-doubt on the other.

—Young (2011, p. 2)

Does Sana's situation sound familiar to you? Perhaps you've experienced similar feelings of inadequacy or isolation in your professional role—or felt, at some point in your career, like an imposter. If so, you're not alone. These feelings are quite normal, and many of us will experience them at some point in our career. Clance and Imes (1978) use the term *imposter phenomenon* (IP) to designate an internalization, particularly prevalent among women, of the idea that they may be intellectually phony. "Despite outstanding academic and professional accomplishments," they write, "women who experience the imposter phenomenon persist in believing that they are really not bright and have fooled anyone who thinks otherwise" (p. 241). You may be more familiar with the term *imposter syndrome*, used similarly. The clinical symptoms most frequently reported in Clance's and Imes's initial study of IP are "generalized anxiety, lack of self-confidence, depression, and frustration related to inability to meet self-imposed standards of achievement" (p. 242). Harvey and Katz (1985) further described IP victims as exhibiting the following three symptoms:

- The sense of having fooled other people into overestimating one's ability
- The attribution of one's success to some factor other than intelligence or ability, such as luck or personality
- The fear of being exposed as an imposter (p. 8)

More recently, Clark, Vardeman, and Barba (2014) conducted a study of IP among college and research librarians. They found that one in eight librarians reported above average IP scores, and librarians who had been working for less than three years had greater imposter feelings than the other participant groups in the study. These librarians attributed their feelings of inadequacy in their professional lives to a variety of factors: lack of support and feedback from a supervisor, negative feedback from others, lack of training, rapid changes in technology, toxic relationships, and unwanted reassignment of job duties (p. 264). This isn't particularly surprising, especially for newly minted professionals or anyone who may feel somewhat intimidated by unfamiliar responsibilities. Lacey and Parlette-Stewart (2017) confirm this, having experienced their own personal struggles with imposter syndrome as new librarians. While mentioning many of the factors listed in the aforementioned study, they also place emphasis on the pressure to contribute to the profession and to fit into the organization—to be taken seriously while feeling trivial, naïve, and ignorant. Some of the strategies that helped them overcome these feelings and become more confident in their roles included employing physical exercise (posture, power poses, etc.); developing a support network with others who were experiencing imposter syndrome themselves; helping onboard new colleagues; participating in association work; and employing positive affirmations, self-talk, and mantras (pp. 3–6).

The first few years on the job or in a new position can be extremely stressful as we acquire new skills, form new relationships, learn to fit in, and attempt to navigate a new culture while at the same time attempting to feel comfortable and capable in our new roles, and *not* feel like an imposter. There are a number of things that can positively impact those crucial first years and help put library and information professionals on a successful path from the get-go. Among these are elements related to communication, professional autonomy, professional development, mentoring or collegial relationships, and time.

- *Communication:* First and foremost, open lines of communication help ensure that we know what's expected of us and can provide us with channels for voicing our own ideas and concerns.

- *Professional autonomy:* A conception of professionalism that endows individuals with responsibility for determining when and how they will carry out their responsibilities, encourages creativity and innovation, generates greater job satisfaction, and allows for self-care by providing flexibility.

- *Professional development:* Training is critical because no one comes into a new job knowing everything they need to know. Structures and workflows and ways of doing things vary by organization and role, so even seasoned veterans need retooling when they land in a new place. Moreover, continued professional development throughout your career can help you keep current with changing systems, technologies, workflows, concepts, and trends.

- *Mentoring:* New professionals—as well as veterans taking on new roles—can benefit from the expertise and real-world experience that a mentor can provide. And, on the flip side of that equation, seasoned practitioners can benefit from the fresh perspectives that a mentee can provide.

- *Networking:* Venturing outside of your organization once in a while to network and collaborate with others—whether these are individuals in similar roles/institutions, or they are members of your local community who support the work of the library—can provide the kind of stability, motivation, and support that you may not even realize you need.

- *Time:* Taking the time needed to find your sea legs is normal. Often, as newness wears off, and the IP sufferers gain confidence in their abilities, the IP fades as well. In addition, find ways to respect your own time—proactively use completion goals and deadlines to avoid compulsive perfectionism—and then make sure you celebrate time well spent (Rakestraw, 2017, p. 475).

You might be lucky enough to discover that the organizational structures of your institution are set up explicitly to support some of these principles.

If the organizational culture at first blush seems to ignore or even devalue the kinds of support you feel you need, don't be too discouraged. Ideal workplaces are few and far between. It may be that a path to pursuing some of these support mechanisms does exist structurally, but how that might work simply hasn't been explicitly laid out for you. Glance back at some of the exercises in Chapter 3 on decoding your organizational culture, to see if you can identify some potential structures or individuals that could help initiate the support you need. There are also certain steps you can take individually to help alleviate or prevent IP:

- If it's not offered outright, ask for feedback or advice from supervisors and colleagues.

- Take the time to identify those things you enjoy doing most, and see if you can find ways to do more of that and less of the other stuff. Even a subtle shift in responsibilities can pay off.
- Find opportunities to insert creativity into your daily routine.
- Take mental and physical breaks; step away from a stressful environment or situation.
- Create a professional development plan for yourself with short- and long-term goals.
- Set goals, and hold yourself accountable.
- Seek outside support from colleagues in associations, professional groups, and other programs.
- Don't be afraid to try new things or test out new approaches, and don't be afraid to fail.
- Reward yourself—not just for succeeding but for trying.
- Keep track of your achievements and the kudos you garner along the way.

Sometimes just realizing how to take charge of the things you *can* control, and beginning to apply effort yourself, will go a long way toward relieving pressure, giving you more confidence, and helping you feel centered and more capable.

Something else that may help bolster your confidence on the job is becoming more aware of the ways certain kinds of experiences at work affect you and thinking about how you respond in those situations. So often, in the heat of the moment, as we run from one meeting to another or transition from one project to another, we lose sight of how events have played out and how we've responded. We come away with a general sense of positivity or a general malaise but miss out on the clarity that can come from taking a reflective glance back at what's happened.

EXERCISE: PEAKS AND VALLEYS

(Adapted from EDUCAUSE [n.d., pp. 4–6])

This exercise helps to increase your awareness of elements of your work that energize you (peaks) and those that drain you (valleys).

1. Think about your career and some events, or projects, or roles that went especially well. Choose a peak moment.
2. What was that moment? In a journal, write a few sentences or phrases to describe it.

3. Now think specifically about what made that moment particularly ener-
    gizing or satisfying, and add a few phrases to describe those aspects
    and the effects of the moment.

4. Repeat steps 1–3 for a second and third peak moment.

5. Do the same for your key valley moments—from events, or projects, or
    roles that didn't go well or were unsatisfying or draining.

6. Individually, address the following questions about these peak and val-
    ley moments in your journal, or team up with a colleague to discuss:

    •   Do these experiences tend to be either 100 percent satisfying or
        unsatisfying, or is there a mixture of both positive and negative?

    •   What kinds of circumstances or events tend to lead up to your
        peaks? Your valleys?

    •   Are there opportunities on the horizon for setting in motion events
        that could lead to another peak?

    •   Are there steps you can take to avoid the kinds of valleys you've
        identified?

    •   Are there measures you can take to help you through the valleys
        with less negative fallout? Or things you could do that might help
        get you back on your feet afterward?

The kind of self-knowledge that can come from a simple reflective exercise like this prepares you to work proactively toward experiences that will
bring satisfaction to your work and helps you recognize ways to respond
more productively, and with more confidence, to less fulfilling areas of
your work.

MINDFULNESS

*Mindfulness provides a simple but powerful route for getting ourselves
unstuck, back in touch with our own wisdom and vitality. It is a way to take
charge of the direction and quality of our own lives.*

—Kabat-Zinn (1994, p. 5)

"Librarians especially are prone to the side effects of professional multitasking," writes Anzalone (2015). "We may not have started out as jugglers, but our jobs now demand that we become adept at keeping many
balls in the air at once" (p. 563). If we think back to the slate of projects
and initiatives on Marcus's plate, for instance, it's easy to see just how apt
the juggler metaphor is. Within the span of three weeks last spring, he

hosted multiple extracurricular events in the library, cofacilitated a college information fair at the main branch of the local public library, and traveled with the "mathletes" team to a regional competition. This was on top of the library workshops, the curriculum meetings, the science fair committee, and advocacy activities related to his most cherished projects. Just thinking about it all can be dizzying. Marcus remains productive on all fronts, in part because of some popular and time-tested time management habits, some of which are described in Chapter 4. But the thing he credits with really keeping him focused and happy is his mindful meditation practice.

Amid our varied days and routines, and the constant interruptions, it can be difficult to slow down and enjoy the small things. Instead, our minds are elsewhere—either lagging behind or worrying about future events that may never come to pass. Of course, this is not just about librarians or other professionals. As the spiritual leader and peace activist Nhat Hanh (2010) points out, most people are not really "present" a lot of the time—their thoughts and preoccupations are elsewhere, distracted by the most recent disappointments or by anxiousness for things to come. Over time, this mental time travel will take its toll—causing frustration and futility and stress that can detrimentally affect our professional and personal well-being. Toward the end of his first year of teaching, Marcus found himself overwhelmed and frustrated. He would waver between second-guessing his own teaching performance and stressing out about some upcoming meeting or presentation. He felt stuck in a self-destructive loop: dwelling almost obsessively on what he'd done poorly, unable to invest properly in the present, and crippled by anxiety of what comes next. This is when an old friend of his from college recommended mindful meditation.

Kabat-Zinn (1994), mindfulness pioneer and founder of the well-known Mindfulness-Based Stress Reduction program (MBSR) at the University of Massachusetts Medical School, defines *mindfulness* as a nonjudgmental awareness of each moment, cultivated by paying attention in specific ways, nonreactively (p. 4). To be nonjudgmental is to suspend the voice in your head that asks, "Is this good or bad? Do I like or dislike this?" (Verhaeghen, 2017, p. 3). To be mindful is to be more aware of life as it happens, to be more deliberate and thoughtful in one's actions, to live in the present, and to take more enjoyment in each and every moment. Meditation, one of the practices most closely associated with mindfulness, allows you to give complete attention to the present moment while quieting and clearing the mind. Verhaeghen (2017), who writes about the cognitive and behavioral impacts of mindfulness, calls meditation "the laboratory, so to speak, in which you learn to develop mindfulness" and refers to breathing meditation, specifically, as a "prime teaching tool" for those developing a meditative practice (p. 6).

EXERCISE: MINDFUL MEDITATION—BREATHING

(Adapted, in part, from Winston [2016])

1. **Before you start, move around a little bit.** Shake your limbs to release tension, raise and lower your shoulders, tilt your head with one ear toward the shoulder on that side, and do a gentle neck roll forward, just until the other ear is over the opposite shoulder.

2. **Find a comfortable place and sit comfortably.** Be aware of your posture but not overly critical.

3. **Close your eyes.**

4. **Pay attention to how it feels to be in your body.** Begin at the top of your head, and gradually scan downward, recognizing and releasing any tension you find, until you reach the tips of your toes.

5. **Allow your attention to shift to your breathing.** Become aware of its rhythm. After the inhale, is there a slight pause before the exhale begins? What about after the exhale? As you feel the air flow in, what is the impact on sensation in your head, your throat, your chest, your diaphragm? What happens as you exhale? Let your attention rest in this rhythm for about four to five minutes.

6. **If you notice your mind wandering, simply take note and refocus.** It's perfectly natural for your mind to wander during meditation, especially if you are new to this kind of practice. When you feel your thoughts stray, gently draw your attention back to rest on the in-and-out rhythm of your breath.

7. **Find yourself in your body once more.** After four to five minutes of breathing meditation, draw your attention back to the top of your head and scan back toward your toes, noticing the sensations.

8. **Take a moment to appreciate the practice.** Gradually bring back into focus your immediate surroundings, and give yourself kudos for making the effort to establish a little mindfulness in an otherwise hectic existence.

9. **Open your eyes.**

This process of leaving the day-to-day hubbub behind temporarily, in order to focus intently on the breath, even for just a few moments, lays the groundwork for the kind of sustained mindfulness that will support professional growth and satisfaction.

Being mindful can be beneficial in a number of ways. First, it helps you shut out distraction—the chatter of speaking and thinking—and opens up a space for focus and concentration (Nhat Hanh, 2010), as illustrated in the previous breathing meditation exercise. It makes room for attending to the "now." Second, although attempts to suppress difficult emotions may paradoxically *increase* internal conflict and stress (and thereby magnify the negative feelings), if you allow problematic emotions to surface and then process them mindfully—with a degree of objectivity—you may find them *decreasing* in intensity. By creating a psychological distance from our negative emotions in a mindful way, we are protecting our self-worth and maintaining emotional stability (Quinn, 2017, p. 28).

In addition, mindfulness helps us avoid passing judgment on ourselves or others and helps us develop, and model, a calm and professional demeanor (Anzalone, 2015, p. 577). As one advocate describes it, mindfulness practice "makes me just a little more patient, I find, a little more willing to listen, a bit more relaxed, and a little more prepared to insert that all-important half-second pause between thought and action" (Verhaeghen, 2017, p. xi). Through mindfulness, we might be better prepared to interact productively with supervisors, colleagues, and patrons—it might just make us better versions of our professional selves. In *The Mindful Librarian* (2016), Moniz and coauthors examine the language typically used to describe mindfulness and suggest using these as prompts for changing the way we think about our work. If, through mindfulness, we strive to be attentive, aware, observant, nonjudgmental, hyperconscious, and reflective in what we do, then our roles, responsibilities, relationships, and research will take on deeper meaning (p. 49). The next time you interact with a patron, student, client, or colleague, think about these words. Slow down, be fully present in the moment, and find ways to incorporate these mindfulness concepts into your discussion or actions.

In their book, *In This Moment: Five Steps to Transcending Stress Using Mindfulness and Neuroscience*, Strosahl and Robinson (2015) discuss the benefits of mindfulness as a highly portable approach that can be used anywhere at any time, identifying five skills to have in your arsenal for potentially stressful workplace situations.

EXERCISE: FIVE SKILLS

(Adapted from Strosahl and Robinson [2015, pp. 169–171])

You may get to the point where this series of five skills will come to mind automatically. In the meantime, this exercise will help you practice and internalize the process.

1. Recall a stressful situation or event from the past, something that caused you to react very poorly, perhaps with negative consequences.
2. In your mind, place yourself back in that moment. You know what really happened, but imagine that you haven't yet responded to the situation. From that perspective, use the following five prompts to journal an alternative narrative—"what would I have been thinking, if . . ."

	Describe what would be going through your mind:
Observe: Realize that this is a moment to pause. Place yourself in the role of observer.	
Describe: Use objective, emotionally neutral words to describe your feelings and those of others involved in a conflict.	
Detach: Work to add some distance or objectivity to your perspective.	
Love yourself: Assess your role in what happened with compassion and understanding. To fail is human. Focus on how to recover. You are not alone.	
Act mindfully: Even if others are increasing their pace and intensity, slow down and breathe. Decide on an intentional course of action in response to the situation.	

With practice, this kind of mindful response can become part of our daily routine. It takes practice, commitment, and repetition to be able to focus our minds, to be aware of how we act and react, how we talk and listen, how we treat others, and how we treat ourselves.

When it comes to implementing mindfulness in the library, remember that this is something that can be practiced anywhere, at any time, alone or in a group setting. In addition to developing a personal professional approach to mindfulness as a librarian, we can develop and implement programming to support mindfulness practices for our various constituents. Workshops, classes, and events have been implemented in all types of libraries to help patrons, school children, students, community members, and library staff experience the benefits of mindfulness and meditation. A public library in Wisconsin, for example, offers free weekly yoga and group meditation classes for the public (Ruhlmann, 2017). A school library in Spain conducts mindful meditation practice with students to calm them down, help them focus, and teach them new ways to respond in difficult situations (Curtis, 2016). And in Massachusetts, an academic library offers a series of mindfulness programs for students and staff, to help them cope during the most stressful times of the academic year and to promote mental, physical, and spiritual well-being (Eberle, 2018). Look for mindfulness programs at local and national conferences. Seek them out online, or start your own, in your own library or professional organization.

SELF-COMPASSION

Self-compassion is a portable source of friendship and support that is available when we need it most—when we fail, make mistakes, or struggle in life.

—Neff and Dahm (2015, p. 134)

You are being self-compassionate when you show yourself the same consideration, respect, and kindness you would show to a good friend or to a library patron who has come to you for help. When you think about it, being kind to others seems like a natural fit for our profession, where respect and understanding are essential to the collegial and service-oriented work we do every day. Interacting with others may be one of the most rewarding aspects of the job but can also be a major cause of stress, at times. No matter how we feel toward an individual, and no matter what state of mind we may be in at that moment, we strive to see the goodness in them and act with kindness and compassion. This doesn't mean that we ignore their faults or the difficulties arising from the situation. We still fully acknowledge these, without focusing on them, without letting anger, resentment, or disappointment get in the way of responding appropriately and professionally. To be compassionate is to respond with understanding and empathy. To be self-compassionate is to apply the same level of support to yourself.

EXERCISE: SELF-APPRECIATION

(Adapted from Neff [2011, p. 274])

1. In the left column, list ten positive attributes you recognize in yourself—the good qualities that you sometimes display or positive actions you have taken.
2. Acknowledge and really appreciate each of these positive aspects.

3. In the right column, take note of the feelings that arise as you consider these things, even if they are uncomfortable emotions, such as vanity, embarrassment, and so forth.

Positive qualities or actions	How does this make you feel?
1.	
2.	
3.	
4.	
5.	
6.	
7.	
8.	
9.	
10.	

Using reflection in this way, to identify personal qualities and positive actions that have played out in the past, helps prepare you to tune in mindfully, in the present, to the ways you embody positive traits day to day. In addition, acknowledging the feelings that arise during this exercise reminds us that we are as prone to discomfort as anyone else—that we're human too.

We can, at times, be judgmental of other people but often reserve the harshest judgment for ourselves—internally castigating ourselves for missed deadlines and opportunities, slow or poor communication, or for not meeting our own (too high) expectations. We may feel ashamed and vulnerable and, at the same time, as if we are the only ones to have ever failed so miserably at [fill in the blank]. In other words, we block out any compassion for ourselves, because we think we no longer belong to the shared human experience. We may feel disconnected, and may purposefully disconnect from others during these times, leading to more emotional distress. Neff (2011), who is recognized as one of the primary researchers on the topic, notes that "we often become scared and angry when we focus on undesired aspects of ourselves or our lives. We feel helpless and frustrated by our inability to control things—to get what we want, to be who we want to be" (p. 62). Rather than assessing our actions as we would those of any other human being—flawed by nature and deserving of compassion and understanding—we see ourselves as isolated paragons of incompetence. But we are all human, and we will all experience failures and feelings of inadequacy at some point in our careers. We are all inter-connected in our humanity and in our imperfections.

Neff (2009) defines three aspects of the self-compassionate frame of mind: self-kindness (replacement of self-judgement with caring and under-standing); common humanity (feeling oneself to be imperfect and human, no more prone to mistakes than anyone else); and mindfulness ("being aware of one's present moment experience in a clear and balanced manner, so that one neither ignores nor ruminates on disliked aspects of oneself or one's life") (p. 212). Stevens and Woodruff (2018) summarize over a decade of research findings by Neff and others to describe some of the contrasting effects of low and high levels of self-compassion. Key negative effects of low self-compassion include depression, anxiety, and neurotic perfection-ism, while individuals with high levels of self-compassion often experience higher self-determination, autonomy, competence, personal initiative, curiosity and exploration, and so forth, among many other traits (p. 10). As Neff (2009) puts it, "Because self-compassionate individuals do not berate themselves when they fail, they are more able to admit mistakes, modify unproductive behaviors and take on new challenges" (p. 213). Don't these all sound like positive attributes for a professional librarian?

EXERCISE: OBJECTIVE AND COMPASSIONATE ADVICE TO YOURSELF

(Adapted from Neff [2011, pp. 35–37])

1. In a journal, write down something that has been bothering you, or something that you don't like about yourself, or something that you fear. Describe it in detail and in depth.

2. Take a step back, and pretend that you are your own close colleague, best friend, or family member. Read the description aloud with the per-spective of that caring other.

3. Turn the page over, and write down what you would tell your colleague, friend, or family member if this was his/her/their problem/issue/fear.

4. Read your advice to yourself aloud, with compassion.

Remember that the definition of self-compassion is that you will become as caring and supportive of yourself as you would be of someone you love. This exercise gets at the heart of what we're trying to achieve. Although it can be very uncomfortable to focus intently on something that makes us feel badly about ourselves, the payoff for changing our perspective, in terms of positive attitude, can be substantial.

Ever since Sana added the management of electronic resources to her already busy workload, she had been feeling overwhelmed and undersupported, struggling with self-doubt and feelings of inadequacy. She felt that she was letting down not only herself but her colleagues and the students and faculty as well, even though several trusted friends in the library community insisted this was not so—that the challenges she was facing were a quite normal part of adjustment to a new role. After spending several weeks in denial, avoiding the issue, Sana knew she had to do something to turn things around. She started taking some of the good advice she'd gotten, telling herself that she would get through this difficult time, and actively seeking out more support from others. Together, Sana and her supervisor came up with a plan to get her the support and training she needed in order to cover her new responsibilities. When she was feeling stressed, she would shut the door to her office, shut out the world for a few moments, and practice breathing meditation. She worked to more habitually respond well during daily interactions with colleagues and patrons, attending to the present moment and reacting and acting more mindfully and with more compassion for both herself and others. All of this helped to calm her mind and her fears, and she finally began to feel more productive and at home in her newly expanded role. It wasn't easy, but over time, and with deliberate attention and practice, these new ways of approaching her work became routine.

EXERCISE: GRATITUDE JOURNAL

1. In a journal, spend a specific amount of time (perhaps start with just five or ten minutes) writing about the pleasant moments, surprises, kindnesses, gifts, and anything else that has happened during the day that made you feel good. Be specific and descriptive and concrete.

2. Set up conditions that can help you make this brief reflection a regular practice. For instance, invest in a quality notebook reserved for the purpose; block out the same time each day; try to do it in the same, comfortable location; and so on.

Recognizing the things that have gone well, whether by your own hand or through the actions of others, helps cultivate positivity, satisfaction, and gratitude and helps us move toward a more productive professional practice.

It can be easy, at any stage in our careers, to say "yes" to too many opportunities, to become too consumed by work, too overscheduled, too overstressed. As Sana realized, situations like this can lead to dissatisfaction, disengagement, and burnout. Others may find that they've become complacent in their jobs, doing what's expected and nothing more, putting in the required hours and heading home, accepting the status quo. Taking steps to increase confidence, mindfulness, and self-compassion can help us better understand, and objectively relate to, our emotions, successes, and failures. It helps us develop a generally more positive outlook, avoid unnecessary conflict, and connect more fully with the world around us and the people in it.

REFERENCES

Anzalone, F. (2015). Zen and the art of multitasking: Mindfulness for law librarians. *Law Library Journal, 107*(4), 561–578.

Clance, P.R., & Imes, S. (1978). The imposter phenomenon in high achieving women: Dynamics and therapeutic intervention. *Psychotherapy Theory, Research and Practice, 15*(3), 241–247.

Clark, M., Vardeman, K., & Barba, S. (2014). Perceived inadequacy: A study of the imposter phenomenon among college and research librarians. *College & Research Libraries, 75*(3), 255–271.

Curtis, M. (2016). Mindfulness meditation in a school library. Retrieved from https://www.ifla.org/node/10132

Eberle, M. (2018). Bringing mindfulness to the academic library. Retrieved from https://www.masslibsystem.org/blog/2018/07/23/bringing-mindfulness-to-the-academic-library/

EDUCAUSE. (n.d.). Creating a professional development plan [PDF file]. Louisville, CO: EDUCAUSE. Retrieved from https://www.educause.edu/careers/special-topic-programs/mentoring/mentee-or-protege

Harvey, J.C., and Katz, C. (1985). *If I'm so successful, why do I feel like a fake? The impostor phenomenon.* New York, NY: St. Martin's Press.

Kabat-Zinn, J. (1994). *Wherever you go, there you are: Mindfulness meditation in everyday life.* New York, NY: Hachette Books.

Lacey, S., & Parlette-Stewart, M. (2017). Jumping into the deep: Imposter syndrome, defining success, and the new librarian. *Partnership: The Canadian Journal of Library and Information Practice and Research, 12*(1), 1–15.

Marden, O. S. (1907). *The young man entering business.* New York, NY: T.Y. Crowell & Co.

Moniz, R., Eshleman, J., Henry, J., Slutzky, H., & Moniz, L. (2016). *The mindful librarian: Connecting the practice of mindfulness to librarianship.* Waltham, MA: Chandos.

Neff, K.D. (2009). The role of self-compassion in development: A healthier way to relate to oneself. *Human Development, 52*(4), 211–214.

Neff, K.D. (2011). *Self-compassion: The proven power of being kind to yourself.* New York, NY: William Morrow.

Neff, K.D., & Dahm, K.A. (2015). Self-compassion: What it is, what it does, and how it relates to mindfulness. In B.D. Ostafin, M.D. Robinson, & B.P.

Meier (Eds.), *Handbook of mindfulness and self-regulation* (pp. 121–137). New York, NY: Springer.

Nhat Hanh, T. (2010). Five steps to mindfulness. Retrieved from https://www .mindful.org/five-steps-to-mindfulness/

Quinn, B. (2017). The potential of mindfulness in managing emotions in libraries. *Advances in Library Administration and Organization, 37,* 15–33.

Rakestraw, L. (2017). How to stop feeling like phony in your library: Recognizing the causes of the imposter syndrome, and how to put a stop to the cycle. *Law Library Journal, 109*(3), 465–478.

Ruhlmann, E. (2017). Mindful librarianship: Awareness of each moment helps librarians stay serene under stress. Retrieved from https://americanlibrar-iesmagazine.org/2017/06/01/mindful-librarianship/

Stevens, L.C., & Woodruff, C.C. (2018). *The neuroscience of empathy, compassion, and self-compassion.* Amsterdam, The Netherlands: Academic Press.

Strosahl, K.D., & Robinson, P.J. (2015). *In this moment: Five steps to transcending stress using mindfulness and neuroscience.* Oakland, CA: New Harbinger.

Verhaeghen, P. (2017). *Presence: How mindfulness and meditation shape your brain, mind, and life.* New York, NY: Oxford University Press.

Winston, D. (2016). A 5-minute breathing meditation to cultivate mindfulness. Retrieved from https://www.mindful.org/a-five-minute-breathing-meditation/

Young, V. (2011). *The secret thoughts of successful women: Why capable people suffer from the impostor syndrome and how to thrive in spite of it.* New York, NY: Crown Business.

7

Discovering Your True Purpose:
Reflective Practice

The development of reflective practice is the pinnacle of professional competence.
                                                    —Larrivee (2005, p. 11)

Camila employs purposeful strategies when it comes to getting things accomplished at work, and reflective journaling is one of her tools. Thinking reflectively helps her feel more in control of the choices she makes, career-wise and day to day. She started journaling in high school to help with her creative writing, jotting down thoughts, ideas, phrases, memories, and bits of overheard conversations. In graduate school she used journaling and reflection to consider ideas similar to those outlined in Chapter 1, to determine career direction, personal strengths, and next steps. On the job, she has built reflective journaling into her weekly routine, asking herself questions about specific challenges of the job, the materials she is processing, cataloging practices, and the ins-and-outs of the professional relationships she maintains. As an example, she keeps a digital (and searchable) list of classification questions that have come up, as a way to help her work out specific solutions and also maintain consistency in description across all of the ongoing projects she oversees. And, in the rare cases where organizational politics seem to be affecting local decision-making, "thinking through" all the issues and major players in writing provides her with more confidence, and calmness, as she navigates the minefield. For Camila, reflection is a powerful tool for improved practice, professional development, and career direction.

Reflection involves close scrutiny of one's own work. Not surprisingly, questioning your own words and actions can be uncomfortable at times. However, through the development of a disciplined, thoughtful, and habitual practice, reflection helps you become more accountable and proactive in decision-making and practice and can provide agency for shaping your own future. In this final chapter, we will explore the meaning of, and purposes for, reflection in a professional context and offer concrete strategies for using this approach to address day-to-day practices and long-term development. We'll also consider the role reflection may play in helping you direct and navigate the future course of your career. If you are new to reflection, you'll be able to work through exercises for getting started and developing reflection as a habitual professional practice. If you are like Camila, and consider yourself a naturally reflective practitioner, or if you already employ reflective thinking in some measure, these exercises may refresh your focus on reflection in a professional context.

Initially theorized in 1933 by the philosopher John Dewey and further developed by thinkers such as Donald Schön (1983), who studied learning within organizations, and education professor Jack Mezirow (1990), reflection involves reviewing and questioning the past and channeling your thoughts in a deliberate and controlled way toward a potentially changed future. In a professional setting, reflective thinking may serve a variety of purposes—for individuals and at the organizational level. It may involve many different activities such as writing and journaling, dialog and discussion, and recording and archiving. Dewey (1998) described reflective thought as the "active, persistent, and careful consideration of any belief or supposed form of knowledge in the light of the grounds that support it and the further conclusions to which it tends" (p. 9). Let's think about this. To be reflective is to focus on what has happened or what is known "in the light of" the assumptions that underlie it and of how it will (or has) impact(ed) the future. Mezirow (1990) differentiates between simple "reflection," involving consideration of our past experiences and actions, and "critical reflection" as something deeper, the process whereby we examine the assumptions *underlying* our actions (p. 1). Amulya (2011) simply states that "the key to reflection is learning how to take perspective on one's own actions and experience—in other words, to examine that experience rather than just living it" (p. 1). There are as many ways of practicing reflective thinking as there are practitioners, and the fluidity and pervasiveness of this practice provide us with various opportunities to consider how reflection might best serve our own professional purposes.

WHY TAKE UP REFLECTION?

By developing the ability to explore and be curious about our own experience and actions, we suddenly open up the possibilities of purposeful learning—learning derived not from books or experts, but from our work and our lives.

—Amulya (2011, p. 1)

Professional competencies that support development of other competencies have been called "meta-competencies," and reflection has been labeled a "super-meta-competency" (Cheetham & Chivers, 2005, p. 109). In general, reflection aims to deliver clearer thinking and action by helping us perceive and evaluate the processes by which we function and learn. Reale's (2017) *Becoming a Reflective Librarian and Teacher* is the most substantial articulation of reflective practice for librarianship to date. Although aimed primarily at teaching librarians, Reale presents an exploration that can support development of reflective practice across the profession. "As professionals—as *human beings*," writes Reale, addressing the purposes of reflective practice, "we get to describe, understand, and improve upon our own process" (p. xii, emphasis in the original). Without reflection, we may tend to respond to problems or dilemmas with "haphazard, reactive patterns of behavior" (Brown & Gillis, 1999, p. 171), which could set off "a cycle of muddled and obsessive thought" whereby the problem itself escapes scrutiny (Reale, 2017, p. 51). Troubling situations are viewed less as crises by reflective practitioners and more as opportunities or challenges to be approached in a controlled, deliberate way (p. 9). It is a process that "shows us to ourselves, reveals and brings to light those aspects of our professional lives that are best dealt with once they have been articulated" (p. 120). Reflective thinking provides benefits not only for us, our colleagues, and the institutions we work for but also for the individuals and communities we serve. For instance, self-reflection foregrounds the habitual ways that teachers respond in certain contexts without even knowing it; it helps them "slow down" in the moment so that they become more aware of how they see and react to students (Larrivee, 2005, p. 18). And research has shown that reflective practice enables nurses to more easily view each patient as a unique individual and to develop and practice empathy (Gustafsson & Fagerberg, 2004). These skills are essential in any service industry.

For some, reflection is one of the things that separates the professional from other types of practitioners. It is a way of knowing that is foundational for being able to think on your feet and employ professional judgment (King & Kitchener, 1994). Reflection allows professionals to consider their own practice from different perspectives and helps them develop the habit of seeking out opportunities for adding new perspectives. "Reflection means seeing a situation in the holistic sense of the word, from all angles, and evaluating ourselves from within that particular situation" (Reale, 2017, p. 25). Reflective journaling over time, for example, "can show transformation, progression of thought, and problem-solving, and enhances a critical stance toward one's practice: the ability to see, in retrospect, what one cannot reasonably understand while in the moment" (p. 24). Sustained, habitual reflection is a form of continual professional development (CPD), which itself is considered "one of the defining characteristics of being a member of a profession, rather than having an occupation or doing a job" (Corrall, 2011, p. 239). With perspective come professional accountability, authenticity, and self-assurance. Larrivee (2005) writes that in examining one's own assumptions and beliefs, practitioners (in this case, classroom teachers) become sensitive to differences between what they say and the actions they take. They become less defensive and more authentic, where "being authentic means not depending on others for your sense of well-being, not having to appear in control, to look good, or refrain from rocking the boat" (p. 13). Over time, the reflective professional begins to incorporate core values into "a deliberate code of conduct that embodies who you are and what you stand for" (p. 15). Thus professional identity, itself, can be grounded in reflective authenticity.

Building on Dewey, reflective practice as a development tool has been cultivated extensively in certain sectors, especially early on in education (e.g., Mezirow, 1991; Schön, 1983) and health care (e.g., Brown & Gillis, 1999; Smith, 1998). Given its history as a major theme in teacher education, it is not surprising that the concept of reflective practice first gained traction in library discourse as a model of professional development for teaching librarians (e.g., Corrall, 2017; Grant, 2007; Jacobs, 2008; Thomas, Tammany, Daier, Owen, & Mercado, 2004). A significant thread in this literature has come from those advocating for reflective practice as a means to help legitimize information literacy as a learning domain within higher education, particularly at a time when challenges to librarians' pedagogical authority were coming from other campus stakeholders (e.g., Jacobs, 2008; O'Connor, 2009; Whitworth, 2012).

We all know that work in the information sector of the twenty-first century can be hectic. Day-to-day challenges and workload seem to increase continually and come at us from all sides. In hectic situations, habit and practiced reflexes take over—sometimes it's the only way to accomplish all that we do. Reale describes this mode of operation as a "fragile house of cards," something we might fear would collapse once we begin adopting reflective practices since that involves questioning how and why we do things the way we do (p. 40). But reflection can be an empowering force for individuals. Research has shown that library professionals use reflective practice to help them identify their own knowledge or skill gaps (Greenall & Sen, 2016) and that library students who complete reflective assignments are in a good position to direct their own professional development and manage career goals, short term and long term (Hallam & McAllister, 2008). Through reflection, librarians address questions about how others see or are impacted by their work, begin to hold themselves accountable, and can take note of changes to their practice over time (Reale, 2017, p. 8). A continuous improvement model is implied in the very concept of reflective practice. Reflective librarians incorporate deliberate consideration of past, present, and future in their approach to self, organization, and community.

Although advocacy for reflective practice in our profession is relatively new, there have been some strong calls for establishing it as an integral part of professional practice in libraries. Corrall (2017) argues for recognition of reflection as a threshold concept in the profession, something that transforms the individual so profoundly as to render reversion to previous modes of practice unthinkable. And reflective practice has also begun to garner official sanction within librarianship. The Chartered Institute of Library and Information Professionals (CILIP), an organization providing professional certification and guidance in the United Kingdom, embeds reflective professional development requirements into its programs for certification and charter membership (Owen & Watson, 2015).

GETTING STARTED

Simply begin. *No excuses.*
—Reale (2017, p. 19, emphasis in the original)

According to Reale (2017), reflective practice requires time, the psychological ability and willingness to face honest self-criticism, and some level of tolerance for risk taking (pp. 6–7). To be honest, the reflective process can be a little intimidating—there are so many ways to "do" it, seemingly each with its own enthusiastic following. What's the best way to begin? Just start, Reale advocates, even if you're not sure you've learned all there is to know about the theory and practice of reflection. You shouldn't worry about getting it "right" (pp. 26–27). There are plenty of reasons to hesitate, but making do with current practice ignores the potential benefits of responding differently the next time that same pesky problem rears its ugly head. "The inconvenient paradox here is quite simply that the busier we are, the more we need reflective practice," writes Reale. "The busier we are, however, the more resistant we may be" (p. 47). Would-be practitioners may be intimidated by the challenge, but sometimes the best way to start is simply to jump right in.

When problematic situations arise in the course of an individual's work, they might notice a certain dissonance or experience an uncomfortable feeling about what went down. In some cases, this dissonance may spontaneously turn that individual into an "active inquirer," as they begin critiquing the situation and thinking of new ways to respond (Larrivee, 2005, p. 11). Even if you have never considered yourself a reflective practitioner, you may recognize this scenario. Heading up a task force of colleagues from across his organization to set up a new data archiving platform, Amir found himself struggling to organize all of the strands of activity involved. Everyone was a little frustrated, and team morale was slipping. After one particularly tense exchange, a colleague of his simply clammed up—refusing to participate in the discussions that were essential for moving the project forward. Amir didn't quite know what to say to remedy the situation and get things back on track, and the meeting sputtered to an end. Back in his office, Amir found himself turning what happened over and over in his mind, knowing he hadn't handled the moment very well. Frustrated and confused, he put pen to paper and outlined what occurred during the meeting. Then he came up with a list of "could have" responses and better ways to have handled the situation. But, since the moment had passed, what should he do now? How could he help his team recover? He kept writing. The page was a hodgepodge of words, phrases, and mixed-up sentences, but eventually his thinking became clearer and less reactionary. A number of possible ways forward presented themselves. It's not uncommon for some kind of challenging situation or incident to provide an impetus for reflective thinking. "A tremendous thing that happens to people when they once discover that putting yourself into that feeling of being confused, that zone of confusion about something very concrete, can lead them to new ideas" (Connelly & Clandinin, 1992, p. 3). In Amir's case, he felt a compelling need before stumbling on the practice of reflection as a possible solution.

Amir sort of "fell into" reflective practice, and it paid off, but that doesn't mean it's easy. As Reale (2017) puts it, "If reflection does not make you squirm, you might not be doing it right" (p. 3). This is a colorful exaggeration, of course, but by its very nature, reflection often comes with discomfort. If you are like Camila, and have been using reflection in some form or another for so long that you've forgotten any challenges or missteps along the way, you may feel fairly comfortable with the initial dissonance, whereas those just getting started, like Amir, may experience frustrating "incremental fluctuations of irregular progress, often marked by two steps forward and one step backward" (Larrivee, 2005, p. 15). And let's face it, there could be real risk involved. For example, Camila and Amir have both employed reflective practices in response to situations that were tricky, either politically or on an interpersonal level, potentially putting at risk the organizational networks they rely upon, their jobs, even their mental and emotional well-being (Brookfield, 1990, p. 178). Also, being willing to face some uncomfortable truths about yourself and your practices, without responding defensively, and being open to the possibility of real change are difficult and necessary parts of the process (Reale, 2017, p. 3). Without honesty, one might end up clinging to old excuses or rationalizations, rendering the entire endeavor futile (p. 25). Simply put, "reflection without honesty is not reflection" (p. 36). Then there's the practicality of it all. As mentioned earlier, Reale (2017) sees the status quo for many busy librarians, whose day-to-day operations rest largely on reflexive practices, as a "fragile house of cards" (p. 40). What happens when we discard the assumptions that have been our foundation? Larrivee (2005) describes an initial "sense of liberation" that is quickly replaced by a "fear of being in limbo." "Old ways of thinking no longer make sense, but new ones have not yet gelled to take their place and you are left dangling, in the throes of uncertainty" (p. 15). Nonetheless she recognizes this stage of discomfort as an important part of the process. Although in the moment it may seem like the worst idea ever, allowing yourself—even temporarily—to fully experience this uncertainty, anxiousness, and confusion opens the door to positive changes in understanding and perception. "If you can weather the storm, you emerge with a new vision" (p. 15).

Reale advises that librarians new to reflection start simply, and for novices a single question or issue may be less intimidating than the holistic concept of reflective practice (p. 37). If you don't currently find yourself in a particularly dissonant or problematic situation, you may want to think about taking up a topic or issue that's been nagging you or preoccupying your thinking (Reale, 2017, p. 27). "Messy" real-life situations, questions without easy answers, and challenges that ask for integration of new and previous learning are also good potential places to begin (Moon, 1999, pp. 175–176). Then it's time to dive in.

If you are a novice, one way to proceed might be to follow the outlines of one of several conceptual models out there that elaborate the stages of reflective practice. Reale (2017) describes a three-phase process of focus, analysis, and action (pp. 40–49).

EXERCISE: THREE-PHASE REFLECTIVE PROCESS

(Adapted from Reale [2017, pp. 40–49])

Focus on a single problem, issue, or incident. Write about this topic, following each of the following three steps in sequence.

1. **Focus:** Just write, until the outlines of the issue begin to clarify.
2. **Analysis:** Keep writing, separating the problem from the emotions that surround it and seeking out and analyzing new information (this may involve consulting with colleagues or other forms of research).
3. **Action:** Continue to write, thinking of the problem from new angles and seeking ways to experiment or resolve the situation.

Using Reale's conceptual model as a guide not only provides an opportunity to try out reflection in response to an incident or issue but it can also help ground the practice in its outcome. There is an assumption that reflection will change you as a professional, that paying attention to the practice will impact you and, by extension, the practice itself. Follow-through is essential, and this is apparent in Reale's final phase.

As suggested earlier, however, there are many, many different ways to employ reflective thinking. Consider trying out some of the approaches listed next, adapted from suggestions in the literature.

EXERCISE: EXPLORING REFLECTIVE APPROACHES

Browse through the approaches outlined next, select one, and begin writing about your reflective topic. You may want to try out a few different approaches to see what seems to work best for you.

Reflective Narrative

(Adapted from Reale [2017, pp. 63–65])

This exercise is designed for reflection on a specific incident that has occurred. Consider the following:

1. Observation: What did you see and hear?
2. What did you think and feel at the time, and how did that evolve?
3. What happened when you tried out different solutions?
4. How has your conception of the problem changed?

Find a New Metaphor

(Adapted from Mezirow [1990, p. 12])

1. Think about how the problem or situation is defined, using metaphor (e.g., *a logistical or political dam that keeps an initiative from moving forward*).
2. Consider alternative metaphors to describe the situation (e.g., *a traffic jam instead of a dam*).
3. How might approaches to resolving the issue change if you change metaphors (e.g., *ways to control and direct traffic*)?

Self-Interview

(Adapted from Reale [2017, p. 58])

Cast yourself as both interviewer and subject:

1. Ask tough, direct questions of yourself about a challenging incident or a situation that made you feel inadequate or uncomfortable.
2. Answer as directly and honestly as possible.

Check Your Filters

(Adapted from Larrivee [2005, pp. 19–22])

1. Thinking subjectively, are any of these things mediating your responses to an issue or situation?
   - Past experiences
   - Beliefs
   - Assumptions/expectations
   - Feelings/mood
   - Personal agendas/aspirations

If the answer is yes to any of these elements, that element can be considered a "clogged filter."

2. For each clogged filter:
   a. What aspect of that area is clogged?
   b. What habitual responses kick in?
   c. What types of responses are "screened out"?
   d. What steps can you take to relieve the clog?

Dialog for Points-of-View

(Adapted from Reale [2017, p. 59])

Write a dialog between yourself and someone else about the situation or issue.

Concept Mapping

(Adapted from Deshler [1990, pp. 343–345])

1. Describe, in visual format, what you know about a topic, without analysis. Include concepts, influences, and relationships among them. Use any medium: paper and pen, post-it notes, and so forth.
2. Reflect: How are individual concepts related to others? Where do you see duplication? What might be missing? Are there contradictions? Does the map adequately represent what you think and feel? What underlying assumptions can you identify? How might using different terminology affect overall meaning?
3. Construct a second version of the map that reflects your analysis.

Lists

(Adapted from Reale [2017, pp. 59–60])

Find a way to itemize any type of elements related to the experience or issue. For instance:

1. Pro and con lists related to an impending decision
2. Steps in a process
3. Different perspectives on an issue

There are probably thousands of different ways to respond reflectively to an issue, incident, or experience. In addition, exploring the use of a variety of modes of expression (dialog, narrative, poetry, drawing, etc.) could more effectively capture the uniqueness of your experience and perspective and perhaps could make reflection seem less effortful (Reale, 2017, pp. 55–56). In other words, this kind of work can be fun!

BUILDING REFLECTIVE HABITS

Regularity with reflective practice builds a muscle, a habit of mind, a way of being.

—Reale (2017, p. 27)

Reflection can be a deliberate means for learning, but it's also a means for getting through the day. As she works with her colleague to clarify terminology used in cataloging a manuscript, Camila is taking note of what is happening in their discussion, in the moment, considering past experience and knowledge in order to determine her actions and responses. We all employ reflection in some form or other—continually, before, during, or after a situation or encounter—and it often takes place without our ever being aware of it. And in our professional spheres, we subconsciously call upon our past experiences all the time. But remember, for Dewey, reflective practice is "active, persistent, and careful." It should be deliberate and habitual; it is a practice that takes practice. Reflective practitioners regularly take time to examine what they have done and how they have come to certain assumptions. This allows us to reconsider "the [otherwise] taken-for-granted" about how we work, learn, and live (Larrivee, 2005, p. 11). The practice must be sustained in order to really effect change, it must involve critical inquiry to have impact on an ethical level, and it requires a sometimes uncomfortable depth of self-reflection so that we can address both our deepest held beliefs and how these affect our interactions with others (p. 10). Critical reflection, in particular, requires intention and effort. Individuals often deny negative experiences or blame their own flawed actions on circumstances or on other individuals; this is a common self-preservation tactic that can keep us from honest self-perception. For this reason, reflection in a professional context is most effective when it is deliberate and planned (Knapp, Gottlieb, & Handelsman, 2017, p. 168). Building a habit takes time. "Have *patience* with the process," Reale urges (2017, p. 28, emphasis in the original).

Beginning to think about reflection as a routine is part of the process of developing a habitual practice. If possible, set aside regular times for reflection—begin with fifteen to thirty minutes a few times each week (Reale, 2017, p. 27). Think about setting up habitual conditions and ways of reflecting, the places and tools that may become second nature (p. 49). Larrivee (2005), writing specifically about reflective journaling, suggests asking yourself some questions; among them are the following: What kind of schedule is realistic? What format(s) or genres of journaling might you try? Would categorizing entries be helpful? (pp. 16–17). To help build a habitual reflective practice, consider planning ahead. Anticipate that your meetings or other daily encounters with others—be they colleagues, institutional stakeholders, or library users—will provide opportunities for reflection after the fact. Reale (2017) suggests slowing down in the moment to take just a few quick notes about the context of what's happening (p. 64).

Exercise: Capture the Context

(Adapted from Reale [2017, p. 64])

If you determine that an experience is ripe for reflection, record some specific elements as the experience plays out. Make note of the following elements, even if you're not sure they'll be important:

1. Date, time, and location
2. Specific circumstance, in a few words
3. How you're feeling, in a few words
4. What the weather is like
5. Any other potentially interesting conditions or details

These data may or may not become relevant as you reflect following the experience, but there's always the chance that patterns will emerge when you find an opportunity to review your reflective notes or artifacts from a greater distance.

Beyond specific encounters or other experiences (unsettling or otherwise), there are plenty of areas of professional practice that could benefit from deliberate reflective thinking, and taking up any of these topics or approaches regularly will support the development of habitual reflection.

Exercise: Exploring Practices to Build a Reflective Habit

"Propulsive" Writing

(Adapted from Reale [2017, p. 56])

1. Free write for a specified (but brief) duration.
2. Even if you've run out of things to say, keep writing for the entire time period.

Daily Reflection

(Adapted from Larrivee [2005, p. 17])

1. Develop a set of just five to six questions relative to your daily practice (as an example, *were there any uncomfortable interactions with students or clients at the reference desk?*).
2. Set up a routine, and respond to these prompts each day.
3. Review periodically to consider routine situations, practiced responses, outcomes, tentative or deliberate new approaches, and so forth.

Case Study

(Adapted from Larrivee [2005, pp. 16–17])

1. Read a one- to two-paragraph description of library practice (perhaps drawn from professional literature).
2. Describe a similar or related situation that might take place in your own context.
3. What kinds of outside information, research, or support might help you evaluate or implement new approaches to this type of situation?

Finally, individuals can use reflective thinking practice to help them develop an understanding of themselves as professionals, review and evaluate career development, and determine new directions or next steps. In addition to the specific reflective exercises for career planning laid out in Chapter 1, consider the following exercises.

EXERCISE: CAREER REFLECTION

Accentuate the Positive

(Adapted from Reale [2017, p. 73])

1. Name a major strength that you possess.
2. What makes that strength important?
3. What is one specific example that illustrates how/why that strength is important?

Metaphor of Place

(Adapted from Reale [2017, p. 62])

1. "Try to conceptualize your literal and figurative place in your library or organization and describe it by comparing it to something else." For

example, *you in the center of the action with others' efforts flowing around you, like a rock in the river rapids.*

2. What does this suggest about how your efforts contribute to the whole? About how others see you?

3. What proactive steps could you take in response, either to solidify your position or to change it?

Aligning Beliefs and Practices

(Adapted from Larrivee [2005, p. 26])

1. Consider a core belief related to your practice, for example, about human nature, learning, or information (e.g., complete the statement, *I believe that patrons learn best when I/we. . .*).

2. List your strategies or practices that align well and support that belief, any that do not align well, and some alternatives for those misaligned strategies.

REFLECTING IN GROUPS

I can say that in my own experience reflective practice is one of the best forms of collaboration available to us.

—Reale (2017, p. 90)

There is a great deal of emphasis in the literature on the value of reflection in solitude. Reale (2017), for instance, talks about "the space that we provide for ourselves" as "the ideal climate for reflecting on our practice" (p. 7). "Being able to reflect in a quiet place, alone and with a notebook," she writes, "is invaluable and certainly the right path" (p. 7). However, for Reale, reflection is also "essentially dialogic" and may productively involve discourse with others as well as with ourselves (p. 32). In groups, individuals may be prompted to clarify their own perspectives. "The 'hive mind,' as some would call it, weighs in, usually in the form of questioning, which helps the person presenting the issue to see it from different angles and to use reframing for clarity" (p. 85). In addition, there are benefits from the cumulative experience in the room. "We want their opinions, we want to know what is true for them in their own experiences and to use those experiences as a sort of counterbalance to our own. . . . This is the type of dialogue that is rooted in experience—yours, mine, and ours" (pp. 45–46). Reflecting in groups helps the library professional avoid isolation (Knapp, Gottlieb, & Handelsman, 2017, p. 168) and also helps make us accountable for the work of reflective practice. Productive group reflection may include challenging each other's beliefs and assumptions, analyzing theory, sharing experiences and strategies attempted, devising new strategies, and providing psychosocial support (Reale, 2017, p. 83).

Reflecting in groups can feel particularly risky. All involved should be truly committed to improvement and open to change; otherwise "the conversation can seem either provocative, accusatory, or in some cases, condescending" (Reale, 2017, p. 86). Reale suggests initiating group reflection only with others who have prior experience with solo reflection so that all involved are to some extent comfortable with the vulnerability inherent in the practice (p. 59). Even then, she suggests, tread lightly. "What could we (gently) ask a colleague or a friend in order to get them thinking in a constructive and productive way, a way that would put them in touch with their inner truth, beyond defending an outdated belief system or a deeply ingrained habit?" (p. 88). Among other strategies, Reale suggests balancing listening with sharing; drawing out reluctant sharers and otherwise doing what you can to balance perspectives in the room; respecting each other's ideas, whether you agree with them or not; and trying not to let an idea shared with the group pass without some acknowledgment (p. 91).

EXERCISE: APPROACHES TO GROUP REFLECTION

Ice Breaker

(Adapted from Reale [2017, p. 90])

To begin group practice for the first few sessions, focus together on something other than librarians' individual work—on some article, book, shared challenge, or new idea in the field.

Critical Incident Reflection

(Adapted from Brookfield [1990, pp. 179–182])

1. Individually, write a description of a significant professional incident.
2. Share in small groups.
3. Within small groups, collaborate to identify underlying assumptions or beliefs that may have shaped the practice described.

Fuel for Individual Reflection

(Adapted from Reale [2017, p. 67])

1. Discuss with the group an issue or problem you have already reflected on.
2. Take quick notes during the discussion.

3. Individually, journal again about the issue or problem, noting not only any suggestions or responses the group provided but also what you think and how you feel about the issue now that other perspectives have been added.

Reflective thinking provides a means for impacting the evolution of professional approaches and practices, the individual's or those more generally in operation within the context of an organization, particularly when you reflect together with colleagues. Not surprisingly, reflective practice across an organization provides an opportunity to collectively "challenge existing overarching structures and our place within and under them" (Reale, 2017, p. 84). In addition, as Reale writes, "The tenets of any profession are both challenged and changed by those who have thought deeply and observed assiduously that profession's present practices" (p. 29). Reflection—individual or collective, wherever it occurs—can have positive impact on the profession as a whole.

REFERENCES

Amulya, J. (2011). What is reflective practice [pdf file]. Retrieved from https://www.researchgate.net/publication/229021036_What_is_reflective_practice

Brookfield, S. (1990). Using critical incidents to explore learners' assumptions. In J. Mezirow & Associates (Eds.), *Fostering critical reflection in adulthood: A guide to transformative and emancipatory learning* (pp. 177–193). San Francisco, CA: Jossey-Bass.

Brown, S.C., & Gillis, M.A. (1999). Using reflective thinking to develop personal professional philosophies. *Journal of Nursing Education, 38*(4), 171–175.

Cheetham, G., & Chivers, G.E. (2005). *Professions, competence and informal learning.* Cheltenham, England: Edward Elgar.

Connelly, F.M., & Clandinin, D.J. (1992). An interview of Donald Schön (on the meanings of reflective practice). *Orbit: Ideas about Teaching and Learning, 23*(4), 2–4.

Corrall, S. (2011). Continuing professional development and workplace learning. In P. Dale, J. Beard, & M. Holland (Eds.), *University libraries and digital learning environments* (pp. 239–258). Farnham, England: Ashgate.

Corrall, S. (2017). Crossing the threshold: Reflective practice in information literacy development. *Journal of Information Literacy, 11*(1), 23–53.

Deshler, D. (1990). Conceptual mapping: Drawing charts of the mind. In J. Mezirow & Associates (Eds.), *Fostering critical reflection in adulthood: A guide to transformative and emancipatory learning* (pp. 336–353). San Francisco, CA: Jossey-Bass.

Dewey, J. (1998 [1933]). *How we think: A restatement of the relation of reflective thinking to the educational process*. Boston, MA: Houghton Mifflin.

Grant, M.J. (2007). The role of reflection in the library and information sector: A systematic review. *Health Information & Libraries Journal, 24*(3), 155–166.

Greenall, J., & Sen, B.A. (2016). Reflective practice in the library and information sector. *Journal of Librarianship and Information Science, 48*(2), 137–150.

Gustafsson, C., & Fagerberg, I. (2004). Reflection, the way to professional development? *Journal of Clinical Nursing, 13*(3), 271–280.

Hallam, G.C., & McAllister, L.M. (2008). Self discovery through digital portfolios: A holistic approach to developing new library and information professionals. Retrieved from http://eprints.qut.edu.au/00014048/01/14048.pdf

Jacobs, H.L. (2008). Information literacy and reflective pedagogical praxis. *The Journal of Academic Librarianship, 34*(3), 256–262.

King, P.M., & Kitchener, K.S. (1994). *Developing reflective judgment*. San Francisco, CA: Jossey-Bass.

Knapp, S., Gottlieb, M.C., & Handelsman, M.M. (2017). Enhancing professionalism through self-reflection. *Professional Psychology: Research and Practice, 48*(3), 167.

Larrivee, B. (2005). *Authentic classroom management: Creating a learning community and building reflective practice* (2nd ed.). Boston, MA: Pearson/ Allyn and Bacon.

Mezirow, J. (1990). How critical reflection triggers transformative learning. In J. Mezirow & Associates (Eds.), *Fostering critical reflection in adulthood: A guide to transformative and emancipatory learning* (pp. 1–20). San Francisco, CA: Jossey-Bass.

Mezirow, J. (1991). *Transformative dimensions of adult learning*. San Francisco, CA: Jossey-Bass.

Moon, J.A. (1999). *Reflection in learning & professional development: Theory & practice*. London, England: Kogan Page.

O'Connor, L. (2009). Information literacy as professional legitimation: The quest for professional jurisdiction. *Library Review, 58*(4), 272–289.

Owen, K., & Watson, M. (2015). *Building your portfolio: The CILIP guide*. London, England: Facet.

Reale, M. (2017). *Becoming a reflective librarian and teacher: Strategies for mindful academic practice*. Chicago, IL: ALA Editions.

Schön, D. (1983). *The reflective practitioner: How practitioners think in action*. San Francisco, CA: Jossey-Bass.

Smith, A. (1998). Learning about reflection. *Journal of Advanced Nursing, 28*(4), 891–898.

Thomas, D.B., Tammany, R., Daier, R., Owen, E., & Mercado, H. (2004). *Reflective teaching: A bridge to learning*. Ann Arbor, MI: Pierian Press.

Whitworth, A. (2012). The reflective information literacy educator. *Nordic Journal of Information Literacy in Higher Education, 4*(1), 38–55.

Index

About the Authors

Susanne Markgren is the assistant director of the library for technical services at Manhattan College, in Riverdale, the Bronx, New York. She has written articles, reviews, and chapters for a variety of publications and is the coauthor of the book *Career Q&A: A Librarian's Real-Life, Practical Guide to Managing a Successful Career* (2013). She serves on the boards of local and national committees, associations, and consortia, and coordinates a mentoring program for the ACRL/NY chapter. She holds a master of library and information science (MLIS) from the University of Texas at Austin and a master of fine arts (MFA) in creative writing from Manhattanville College.

Linda Miles is an assistant professor and librarian at Eugenio María de Hostos Community College—City University of New York. She previously served as public services and user experience librarian at Yeshiva University, and she began her career in the library of Lincoln Center Institute for the Arts in Education. Recent publications include "Egalitarian Teams in Action: Organizing for Library Initiatives," *Urban Library Journal, 32*(2), 2017. Linda received an early-career librarian scholarship from the Association of College and Research Libraries (ACRL) (2017) and an Institute of Museum and Library Services (IMLS) Laura Bush 21st Century Librarian Scholarship (2009–2011). She holds a master of library science (MLS) from St. John's University and a PhD in theater history and criticism from the University of Texas at Austin.